AF613221

Metaverse Investing

The Step-By-Step Guide to Understand Metaverse World and Business, Virtual Land, DeFi, NFT, Crypto Art, Blockchain Gaming, and Play To Earn

Darell Freeman

Cryptosphere Academy

Copyright © 2022 _ Darell Freeman

All rights reserved.

No one is permitted to reproduce or transmit any part of this book through any means or form, be it electronic or mechanical. No one also has the right to store the information herein in a retrieval system. Neither do they have the right to photocopy, record copies, scan parts of this document, etc., without the proper written permission of the publisher or author.

Disclaimer

All the information in this book is to be used for informational and educational purposes only. The author will not, in any way, account for any results that stem from the use of the contents herein. While conscious and creative attempts have been made to ensure that all information provided herein is as accurate and helpful as possible, the author is not legally bound to be responsible for any damage caused by the accuracy and the use/misuse of this information.

TABLET OF CONTENTS

INTRODUCTION

The metaverse did not just start recently; the idea has been around for a long time. In 1992, Neal Stephenson wrote a novel called Snow Crash. The novel describes a virtual world where people go to escape reality. Another novel released in that era with some features of a metaverse is Neuromancer, created by William Gibson. The novel describes a virtual world known as the matrix.

In Snow Crash, the metaverse refers to a 3D space that can be accessed using virtual reality (VR) goggles and personal terminals. The goggles are similar to VR headsets, Oculus Quest, and other models. For those in the game, the 3D space is an environment that has a road called the Street. Like the street we have in our world today, developers can introduce parks, signs, buildings, and special areas where people can visit to engage in battle.

The rules present in the real world do not apply to the metaverse. When players are killed in the metaverse, they have a chance to start over again. This was the idea of Stephenson, which has been implemented in most online games with multiplayer support. Another game, Second Life was launched in 2003 where players can have their avatar, interact with other players, own digitalized property, trade products, and produce virtual items.

Second Life is an upgrade to the initial picture painted of the metaverse; most people described it as a prometaverse. This digital world that exists on its own. The citizens as well the digital assets, can never leave the place.

According to the CEO of Meta, Mark Zuckerberg, the company is creating something bigger than the internet. Zuckerberg made this announcement to the employees of the company some months back.

We'd see a step-by-step guide about the metaverse world and business in this book. Happy reading

CHAPTER ONE: All about Metaverse

Definition of the Metaverse

The metaverse refers to an operational network of 3D digital worlds that can be experienced by a large number of people simultaneously and persistently. Data such as history, entitlements, identity, communications, payments, and objects will be saved to allow for continuity in the metaverse. This is a virtual space where individuals can carry out invention and exploration with other users.

For instance, an individual can enter the virtual environment, visit a shopping mall and buy a digital item that can be sold later for a good price. To see how this will look, picture the movie Ready Player One that was released some years back. However, one difference is that the movie had one major virtual world. The metaverse will have several virtual worlds and perhaps more advanced technology.

Properties of the Metaverse

If the metaverse should become the "new internet," then it must possess certain properties, and they include:

1. Data continuity
2. Unlimited number of users
3. Every individual must have a sense of presence
4. Interoperable
5. Synchronous
6. 3D virtual worlds

What Will Power the Metaverse?

One must be wondering how a digital world with various components and features will be powered. The technology that will power the metaverse includes hardware and software tools, applications, platforms, cloud infrastructure, and user-generated content. These are the technical requirements that will ensure data continuity. Different areas of the metaverse that will be powered by technology are research, education, gaming, social interactions, commerce, and entertainment.

Currently, the framework on which the internet is built can allow many people to tune in for a virtual concert or show. An example was when about 12 million players went to a virtual-reality concert on Fortnite. This infrastructure is impressive but will not support the metaverse. There has to be an improvement for the current infrastructure to support the digital world.

Hardware such as virtual-reality headsets will also be needed to enhance the appearance of avatars and the environment in 3D. One of the major producers of such headsets is Meta. Meta is the producer of the famous VR headset, Oculus. Other companies such as Microsoft and Apple are also showing support for hardware that will be used in the virtual world. Apple is rumored to be making plans to release its VR and AR headsets this year.

In the Metaverse, users will utilize traditional devices such as mobile devices and computers and then improve their experience with immersive VR and AR wears. More also, blockchain technology, which started in 2009, can also be leveraged to ensure data continuity. Non-fungible tokens or NFTs are mostly called paint a vivid picture of how the blockchain network can help verify digital assets. Some three-dimensional VR platforms are already taking advantage of blockchain technology.

When Will the Metaverse Arrive?

There has been a lot of craze concerning the metaverse with different companies interested in the digital world. How long are we going to wait before we begin some of the projects these companies have been working on. It is no news that several platforms like Roblox are already giving users a feel of what the metaverse wil be like, but this is far from what we should expect. Zuckerberg believes the metaverse will come at the decade's end, but it could be faster since different organizations are putting infrastructures in place.

What is the difference between the internet and the metaverse?

Several persons have been asking questions since news about the metaverse started flying around. Will the metaverse replace the internet? Is the metaverse the next phase of the internet? Will the internet and the metaverse complement one another? Long before the metaverse, the internet has been in existence. Logically, one would need the internet to access the metaverse but are there any notable differences?

What is the Internet?

By definition, the internet refers to a global network with millions of computers, electronic devices, and servers that help facilitate communication worldwide. With the aid of the internet, one person in one part of the world can reach out to another person somewhere else on the globe. There is a lot that the internet can be used for. The only requirement is a computer and then access to the internet. When an individual is online, that means they are connected to the net using a laptop or phone.

Before a network connection can be established, people should know that the internet is simply a network of cables, including TV cables, fiber optical cables, and copper telephone wires. Wireless networks such as 5G, 3G/4G, and WI-FI rely on cables to use the internet.

The moment a computer is used to open a website, the computer sends a series of requests through the wires to the server, where information related to the site is stored. It is like accessing the information stored on the hard drive of a computer. After getting the request, the server gets the information of the website to send it to the computer. All these operations take place within a matter of seconds, depending on how fast your internet connection is.

What is the Metaverse?

As we stated earlier, the metaverse is a collection of technological elements, including augmented reality and virtual reality, where the users enter into a digital space.

In simple terms, the metaverse is a digital space that has digital representations of things, people, and places. In this digital world, real people are represented by characters and avatars. Neal Stephenson coined the term "metaverse" in his book "Snow Crash." Stephenson imagined a world where real people took up life avatars and met in 3D buildings and VR environments that were realistic.

What Is the Distinction Between the Metaverse and the Internet?

People are either on social media chatting with friends, playing a game, streaming videos, or just on a website when it comes to the internet.

With the metaverse, their actions are taken a step further. The user is placed at the center of the whole scene. That is one thing that makes the metaverse stand out from the internet. The metaverse combines various parts of augmented reality, virtual reality, physical reality, artificial intelligence, online gaming, NFTs, cryptocurrencies, and social media. Users can now interact with all these things virtually as if there are there. These realities are what make the internet and the metaverse concepts different.

The metaverse is the gateway to a realistic and stronger experience, while the internet is nothing compared to it. To get a feel of what the metaverse looks like, users can try out Fortnite.

Another major difference between both concepts is their purpose. Users can be online but not interact with anyone using the internet, while the metaverse is all about digital interaction. When a person is in the metaverse, there has to be interaction either with the environment or other people around work, beach, exercise, school, etc. Individuals who have strong beliefs about metaverse believe it will bring connection between friends and remove the barrier of communication. Friends can now visit concerts, conferences, and virtual trips around the world together without being there physically. This is similar to what Zuckerberg said, "the metaverse gives you the feeling of being there with someone else and removes the barrier of distance."

As for the internet, the device is the main point of attention for the internet, but this is different from the metaverse. Online interactions have become multi-dimensional in the digital world. More than using VR headsets for gaming, they can offer a much wider experience in the virtual world. Markets, countries, planets, superheroes, beautiful sites will share one universe. It is claimed that the metaverse will bring unity to mankind.

One thing is for sure, and there will be numerous opportunities on the metaverse. The virtual economy will consist of different sections ranging from clothing, gaming, recreation, cooking, and more. Just imagine what the opportunities would be like. For better user experience, mobile phones, computers, and the internet will have to be faster in operation and stronger.

For decades now, the internet has been a crucial part of our lives. Will this be the same for the metaverse? Although many believe the metaverse will replace the internet, that is not true. The internet, in truth, will be needed to access the metaverse. So, it is not necessary for people to do any with the internet as it Will be needed to share new experiences, virtual spaces, and holograms.

Difference between web 3 and the metaverse

Definition

This is the first consideration before we can fully differentiate both terms. The metaverse is a virtual world where people can interact with 3D objects in a virtual space. Using virtual reality headsets, the virtual world will allow users to interact with the environment, object, and people.

Web 3.0 is simply changing the systems or approaches through which individuals can control online identities and digital assets. Using web 3.0, individuals can create any content that they like, have control over it, and still sell the content. Having said this, a web 3.0 is a concept that is being developed for the next generation of internet users where they can exercise ownership and power over whatever they can create.

The Underlying Technology

Another factor to consider in the comparison is the kind of technology they are based on. As for the metaverse, it has different important technologies that enable the entire system to work. They are decentralization, experiences, creator economy, interfaces, connectivity, and the needed technological tools to develop the metaverse.

Web 3.0 is centered on inventing a decentralized web that only depends on cryptocurrencies and blockchain. Blockchain will help its users communicate and interact with services online under the control of a decentralized computers system. Also, web 3.0 can even use the functionalities of the public blockchain to allow open and direct access to individuals that have an internet connection.

Scope of Applications

This is another factor to consider, and it will draw reference to the applications. The metaverse is an innovation that brings education, movies, entertainment, social platform, gaming, and simulation-based training all in one environment. However, all these applications within the metaverse are still being developed and not yet ready to be launched. Hence, it is still soon to assume the platform will be able to handle all these activities in the virtual world.

Web 3.0 is a standard for a new generation of internet users. It can be referred to as a set of regulations that would apply to all internet users. As a result, it would apply throughout the entire web and not for a specific set of applications.

Why Does the Metaverse Involve Holograms?

At the onset of the internet, there were some technological innovations such as sending information over long distances or moving from one page to another using hyperlinks. These features served as a foundation on which the internet was built. It was upon these structures that the present-day internet was built. Now, more features and structures have been introduced to make life easier and better. Some of these structures include social networks, apps, websites, and lots more. Also, some accessories and facilities are not tied to the internet but are needed to make using the internet smoother. These accessories include a mouse, touchscreen, displays, keyboards, etc.

As for the metaverse, structures, facilities, and features will have to be put in place first before improvements can be made. These structures include motion-tracking sensors and tools that can tell what direction a person is looking at or where their legs are, or the ability to have lots of people at an event under one server. Hopefully, the metaverse will be able to host millions of people in real-time in the future. These new structures and technologies will make the Metaverse experience fun and worthwhile.

However, some limitations may arise that might be difficult to overcome. During most Meta adverts, especially those sponsored by tech companies such as Microsoft, you will see a video of people interacting and having a good time in the metaverse. That's what is shown in most commercials. The facilities that will be used to access the metaverse are still a topic for discussion. Take a look at the VR headsets; most people are still uncomfortable putting them on. While some develop a headache after using it for a long time, others have motion sickness. Also, augmented reality glasses are not any better. People have similar issues when they use them. Moreover, no one has figured out how people will use these headsets or glasses without looking funny in public.

Most companies bypass this issue during their commercials is to show holographic images of people using the metaverse. Many people believe that such an illusion is not possible as it will require very advanced forms of technology that are unavailable. In most movies, such holographic displays are projected through augmented glasses or watches, but that is not attainable in reality at the moment. Making a 3D picture appear in midair will require advanced tech.

The demo of how the metaverse will look poses more questions than answers; there is a demo of a person floating through space. One would imagine if the person was sitting on a chair or had to be tied to an aerial rig to pull off such a stunt. For demos that depict a holographic image of a person, is the person using a headset? If they do, how was their face scanned? How will people hold things in the metaverse? Several questions will need to be answered.

At some point, these companies, Meta and Microsoft, are only trying to depict how the metaverse would like using these demos. They are not accounting for every form of technology that will be required. Perhaps, they are developing tools that will make such demos a reality.

If the issue of using AR and VR headsets is solved, people are not comfortable using them regularly. Perhaps, the idea of a floating hologram, playing games at the beach, and having customized avatars would be possible. If tech companies can create a standard for digital avatars, that may rule out the need for headsets. The standard can have characteristics such as fashion style, hairstyle, eye color, type of nose and ear, the color of hair, etc. With the features, individuals will develop their avatars to suit their tastes.

Everyone may not welcome the idea of using headsets or glasses to enjoy the metaverse, but this can be averted if the holographic display becomes a reality.

Many persons consider the metaverse as the evolution of VR as it blends the digital and physical into a common space. As stated before, headsets will be used to access the metaverse, but new technology may be invented to make things better. One way would be to bring the metaverse into the physical world with holographic images. For instance, the holographic image of a friend far away can be teleported directly to your house. That's where holograms come in, but we have a long way to go before we get to that stage.

Metaverse predecessors

Before the metaverse project started taking form, some other devices or platforms could provide one with a digital world feel.

Virtual reality

Most people still think this is the Metaverse, but it is not. This will be part of the metaverse as a tool for entering the digital space. VR headsets will grant people access to the metaverse. This is an environment generated by a computer with objects and scenes that appear real. The individual feels like there are in a particular space when their physical body is in the research world. To enter this environment, a device known as a VR headset is needed.

Gamers also use virtual Reality to feel what it is like to be in the game and by health surgeons to learn surgery. In VR, the computer makes use of math and similar sensors. What the headset does is position the eyes of the user straight inside the digital world. Once the user turns the head, the environment will change accordingly. This makes the world interactive and not just fixed. Virtual reality is experienced using the sense of hearing and the sense of sight.

Fortnite and Roblox

These are two online games that are free to play. These platforms have a large fanbase that is popular among gamers. The developer of Roblox is Roblox

Corporation, while Epic Games developed Fortnite. Fortnite is very popular among teenagers and adults.

Many persons have hyped the game as a forerunner of the metaverse, and they are not wrong. Both games meet up some of the criteria for a digital world. They have special spheres where different avatars exist. Apart from gaming, both games have an economy and various live event.

The only drawback is that avatars in Fortnite cannot be used In Roblox or another digital world. The currency accepted for payment differs for both of them. No form of sexual content is allowed on Roblox. Some popular games on Roblox include Jailbreak, and murder mystery 2

Differences Between Roblox And Fortnite

The players on Roblox are more than those on Fortnite. Players on Roblox are allowed to build their games to suit their choice using Roblox studio. Roblox has bad single and multiple player features. On Fortnite, the game is full of action.

Why the Metaverse Matters

Apart from being in the digital world and having fun, does the metaverse have any other thing to offer? Companies are making a huge investment into the metaverse: so it must be something worthwhile

Five Reasons Why the Metaverse Is Such a Big Deal

1. It might be the next internet

Apart from the metaverse dream that is everywhere at the moment, another concept is gaining momentum: Web 3. Web 3.0 is closely linked to the metaverse. Zuckerberg has referred to the virtual world as the next embodiment of the internet. The metaverse might be the one place where users all over the world will meet up to talk, play, buy, sell, and work. At first, it will start as an option for social media and will eventually cover the entire universe.

2. There Is so much work and collaboration going on in the metaverse. As of 2020 alone, the adoption of virtual reality headsets increased during the lockdown. Companies such as Spatial that hosted meetings witnessed a 1000% spike in usage overnight, and Facebook released its headset known as Oculus. Many persons switched from Zoom to VR/AR-enabled environments because they got tired of zoom sessions which brought a feeling of loneliness. The workplace's degrees of engagement and discussion were no longer there in the Zoom

meetings. The VR-enabled work environment offered people an opportunity to interact with others and the environment rather than staring down on a screen.

3. There are many investment opportunities for those who want to get a cut out of the gains the metaverse will produce. A new economy is on its way now that it is starting on a new level. For developers and creators, this means a way to get more money. Also, the possibility of having an economy that will be run using cryptocurrency will allow users to make more money for themselves when they sell digital assets and nfts on the metaverse. The action is just getting started, and the playing field is leveled. According to experts, the metaverse offers a Trillion dollar opportunities for investors. Apart from business opportunities, Jon will also be opportunities as people will be needed to develop the metaverse. Facebook has promised to create over 10,000 jobs as part of its vision to develop the metaverse. Nike has hired designers to create a digital version of its shoes for the platform, Nikeland.

4. There will be a lot of regulatory and legal Implications. Presently, the issue of cybercrime, privacy, data rights, regulations is part of the conversations surrounding the metaverse. Though

the virtual world will be exciting, there have to be regulations to ensure that cybercrime doesn't creep into the metaverse. NFT fraud is one such crime that is possible. How will the issue of land rights be? The issue of data rights is also another issue. Will it be possible for user data to be stolen? That is why the metaverse is a big deal and has to be given the necessary attention.

5. We are inches away from attaining a virtual world

Presently, not everyone may have heard about the metaverse, but that is about to change soon as operations are in full gear to make this dream a reality. All the structures, infrastructures, technology, and facilities needed to kick-start the virtual world are being produced. According to Zuckerberg, the metaverse will be here in the next decade, which is not very far away. It's creating a lot of buzzes and talk on social media with many people so eager to see how things turn out; this is why it's a big deal.

What about privacy, safety, and mental well-being?

This issue has raised concerns all over the world. Presently, there is privacy and safety issue in the real world concerning the use of the internet. Apart from the problem of fraud, there is also the issue of data theft. These issues have not gone away in the real world and will certainly creep into the metaverse. Since most persons will be living on the metaverse, their social well-being becomes a matter of concern. At the moment, the internet has become an addiction for so many people; how are we sure the metaverse will not pose a greater threat. The metaverse will have access to all the avatars' activities, likes, and dislikes as they interact in the metaverse.

The problem of privacy, security, and safety has to be discussed from the start before these technologies are open to the public for usage.

According to research, making all aspects of one's life now virtual activities will affect the mental well-being of such individuals. Many persons will choose virtual relationships over physical connections. People will not travel long distances to see friends and families. Workers may stop going to their physical workplace.

Some highlighted issues that might be faced in the metaverse include privacy issues, data theft, suicide, bullying, mental health, etc

The Metaverse will bring new challenges and even aggravate the existing challenges. Humans need physical contact and interaction for emotions and feelings to be intact. If it becomes possible for people to stay indoors and do what they want, the physical connection will begin to go away.

The way these tools are built, they are meant to be addictive because these big companies sponsoring such projects will make money when the influx of people into the metaverse is high. We are still battling the problem of addiction associated with web 2.0, and web 3.0 is already on its way. There are fears that such innovation will cut off people from reality and make them more isolated

That is not to say that the metaverse will not be beneficial to all, but it seems the cons will surpass the pros in the long run. Certain issues must be addressed before introducing them to the world. Individuals are advised to learn from what social media has done in the past years and know how to be cautious in the metaverse.

Risks to people

Since these are new technologies, there will not be time to study their long effects before releasing them to the public. The technology will be released without adequately studying the long-term effects it will have on people's minds, health, level of interaction, and brain activity. From numerous studies, prolonged usage of screens and virtual reality headsets can lead to discomfort, dizziness, and cybersickness.

The physical damages

People using virtual reality headsets or glasses can become disorganized in the real world and hurt themselves. Putting on these electronic devices for hours will affect the human mind. They can even start to carry out activities in the real world that will kill them thinking they are in the virtual world. Examples of such activities include jumping off a cliff, walking on the road, and others. These activities can make them insensitive to the hazards in the real world.

Mental health

These new techs have not undergone long-term studies for possible side effects. Usually, the result will vary from person to person. Some effects of spending so much time on games include lonely behavior, depression, violence, suicide, isolation, etc.

Digital consent

Will some laws will set physical boundaries in the metaverse. The laws in the metaverse will have to suit it since it's a digital world, and we may see new kinds of crime emerge. Will there be responsible for actions in the real world?

Data security

Since information is stored in a digital form, how safe is this information? This raises concern over the issue of confidentiality and intellectual property theft. Personal data, financial and emotional data can be stolen

Data and cybersecurity

The places where people can be attacked will be increased. Will the different companies in the metaverse be under any form of regulations? How will these regulations be made?

Identity

If avatars are used as a source of recognition in the metaverse, the person's details can be stolen, copied, manipulated, or even erased. One methods of solving this will be to use biometric identification. Imagine a situation where a bot enters into the metaverse and steals a person's identity. The bot can damage the platform, thereby damaging the person's reputation.

The Challenge Of a 'Perfect' World

Many people are looking for how the work can benefit them because they believe more benefits. People forget to study the harmful effects of what spending time with such technology can bring about. People would live in a world that seems perfect in the virtual space while there is a problem in reality.

No one studies the kinds of long-term impacts people will have spending time in a world where everything's perfect. You've got people struggling in their daily lives, looking at the social media platforms, and they're comparing themselves to the other people. The metaverse would bring up the sign of her for advertisement. It is easier to adopt the 4k method than stop being with Blockchain.

Just type the kind of job you are looking for and the coin. You can also type the title of the job you want to fill in for and then search. It is important to have better-looking characters than poorly made avatars. Soon, the challenge is going to shift. Life will be about where people spend their time, and people in the world can be goal-theme. Nobody knows how the real thing.

What do you believe the metaverse will entail for you?

There is this assumption that we are being sucked into a virtual world, and with time, we would want to spend more time in the virtual world than the physical method. It's helpful for companies to look at the matter ethically to develop strategies that would work than just setting out with anything without thinking about the consequences. No one is showing concern about the things that could go wrong.

Virtual interactions can be harmful to a human living in the virtual world as well as in the real world. One thing about harmful practices is that they spread very fast and usually have long-term effects that can or cannot be reversed. Everyone is talking about the metaverse everywhere you look. There are some building blocks of mental health, and they are social support, sleep, positive relationships, and physical activity.

If you take a look at a technology, whether new or old, the question is not the time people spend on it but the way they use it. Is it promoting good health or inhibiting it. If using the metaverse replaces behavior that is healthy and good for mental health, then it is harmful.

Examples of healthy behavior include healthy sleep, appropriate exercise, relationships with people, and time spent in natural environments. According to Nick Allen, a professor of psychology at the University of Oregon, these technologies will increase good and bad things about social connection.

Will the Kids Be Alright?

The first set of people who get fascinated with new things are young people. They are the adopters of recent technological advancements. Most effects of the metaverse will depend on how dedicated and mindful we are to correct them. The issue now is that these platforms are not designed with safety or development in mind. Another problem we see most times is that the technology itself is not harmful but it's the anxiety, the conflict and rift it causes within families. In order to reduce the anxiety and conflict, there has to be proper attention and design paid to the young user.

The Danger Of Preferring Virtual Life

The metaverse promises to be fun packed and you can imagine what will happen when people start using the metaverse to avoid real life problems or situations. The internet is a very social place and a place for isolation. There are different activities that can be done by done on the internet from social networking, playing of online games, streaming videos. All these are social activities even if there is no direct interaction with other persons.

This will not be different in the metaverse. What we should be scared of is the balance. It is possible for people to stretch preferring the virtual spaces over the physical places because of the kind of accommodation they provide. An avatar can be tall or short, skinny or fat depending on what the individual wants. If people start preferring the virtual life, that may affect people's ability to interact in the real world negatively. It could be social anxiety, lack of self-confidence or belonging.

CHAPTER TWO: Who and what will power the metaverse?

Apart from how the metaverse will become a reality, there are other critical questions the internet society is asking: who will be in charge of the metaverse? Will it be a centralized or decentralized system?

Just like no one owns the internet, nobody would be in charge of the metaverse or be able to claim ownership of it. Certainly, there would be many companies that will form part of the major players in the virtual world such as Microsoft, Unity, Meta, Roblox, Epic Games, etc. This is the reason such companies are spending billions in making the dream a reality.

One thing is sure when the Metaverse is launched, there would be huge competition among the big players. They will try to outshine one another so they can have more persons visiting their virtual space. This is good news for everyone as this will hasten the speed of development. Various companies will want to dominate the digital world and stay at the top for as long as they can.

The Battle for the Metaverse

Facebook, the social giant will try to control most of the time people spend on the metaverse by ensuring they are on their platform. This will generate huge revenue for them. On the other hand, some newcomers would want to build a wide ecosystem of individuals that will build monuments and beautiful sites on the metaverse. With the aid of blockchain, the newcomers will seek ways to ensure the platform is interoperable and decentralized. Individuals will be able to own digital assets and value will be shared among those who work towards developing the system.

What Will Power the Metaverse?

A virtual world that is so complex and multi-dimensional will need to be powered by different kinds of technology for it to operate optimally. Examples of such tech include software tools, applications, hardware, platforms, and user-generated content. In addition, some of the sections that will be present in the metaverse include research, education, gaming, entertainment, commerce, and social interactions. These sections will be powered by different kinds of hardware and software.

Major Technologies that will Power the metaverse

For users to have the best out of the metaverse, companies will have to adopt new-age technologies such as VR, AR, artificial intelligence (AI), 3D reconstruction, and the Internet of Things (IoT).

Blockchain and crypto

Blockchain technology has been around for years now. It provides a transparent and decentralized solution that will allow for accessibility, digital collectability, interoperability, proof of digital ownership, governance, and transfer of value. As for cryptocurrencies, they will allow users to socialize in the virtual world and to send value.

Cryptocurrency can be used if a player chooses to purchase virtual land in Decentraland. The lands purchased will be in form of NFTs. To buy land in Decentraland, the currency needed is MANA. Blockchain technology will allow for the protection and establishment of virtual property.

Years from now, there might be the opportunity of having job opportunities on the metaverse. People will be paid for working in the virtual world using crypto. Companies may end up taking the offices online to allow for remote workers. Such jobs will be metaverse-based jobs.

Augmented reality (AR) and Virtual reality (VR)

This technology enables users to have a fun-filled life three-dimensional experience. It is through these hardware devices that people will enter the metaverse. Virtual reality is different from Augmented reality.

Augmented reality uses digital characters and elements to simulate the actual world. Also, it's very accessible compared to virtual reality. AR can be accessed using digital devices or a smartphone that has a camera. Users can look around and feel their surroundings using interactive digital visuals through the applications. This is similar to the game called Pokemon Go. When a user opens the camera, Pokemons can be seen in the real world

As for virtual reality, the mode of operation is different. It is almost similar to the metaverse. Users can explore its various sections using sensors, gloves, and VR headsets.

AR and VR show the working mechanism of and is move. VR creates a digital society where a different section of the economy is open for investment. VR is making attempts to begin talks concerning crypto. Users have been lonely before the metaverse. Users can sense, hear, and interact with people from all over the world.

Artificial intelligence (AI)

In recent years, artificial intelligence (AI) has been widely used in our daily lives. Recently, AI experts have been researching the possibilities of using AI to create immersive metaverses.

AI has the potential to process massive amounts of data at breakneck speed. AI algorithms, when combined with machine learning techniques, can learn from previous operations, taking into account historical data to produce unique outputs and insights.

None-player characters are always going to be part of every gaming society. NPCs are important for every game because they are at the receiving end of the player's actions and activities. Using artificial intelligence, NPCs can be assigned to differ to sectors to do some tasks or communicate with users. Several players can use the NPC even in different languages compared to a human user.

Another possible thing that AI can be used for is the creation of avatars for use in the metaverse.

Artificial intelligence can analyze two or three-dimensional images to get avatars. The avatars will look more accurate and realistic. To add spice to the whole scenario, AI can create different clothes, hairstyles, and features to enable them to look good.

3D reconstruction

Three-dimensional technology will be used for reconstruction in the virtual world. This tech became popular during the lockdown mostly in the real estate business so potential buyers could see what they want to pay for. Hence, 3D reconstruction was asked to create a virtual property. This same technology will be adopted in the metaverse.

One major challenge faced by the metaverse project is the creation of a digital environment that would be almost similar to what is obtained in real life. Using 3D reconstruction, natural and realistic architectures can be built. The pictures of physical objects will be taken using high-tech 3D cameras and replicated in the virtual world using 3D spatial data and computers. This would mean any object in the real world can be seen in the virtual world.

Internet of things (IoT)

In 1999, this concept was introduced. IoT refers to a system that transforms physical objects and other things in HR physical world and connects them straight to the internet using devices and sensors. When these objects have been connected to the internet, they become a special identifier and can now send and receive information. Presently, IoT is used to connect medical devices, thermostats, and more things to the internet.

One application of this technology in the digital world is the send data from the physical world and send it to the metaverse. The virtual world will be connected to real-life objects that will allow for real-time simulation. Artificial intelligence and machine learning could be used to manage all the collected data.

Who is going to pay for it, and how?

The metaverse is a multi-dimensional project that will need a large amount of money to establish. The reason is that the technological tools present in this age need to be improved to have the capacity to run the virtual world.

Though a universal metaverse has not been developed that will allow users to move from one virtual world in the metaverse to another, various sectors of the metaverse are now popular. This shows that there are numerous options that investors can key into.

The metaverse has different categories that will need funding so that they are developed. Below are the categories that will need funds.

1. Networking
2. Computing power
3. Hardware
4. Virtual platforms
5. Payments
6. Assets
7. Content

These categories were highlighted by the CEO of Tiv. The current market for the metaverse is hot because several companies are keying into the idea. This could lead to some tension.

Who will fund the metaverse?

As we stated earlier, the metaverse does not belong to anybody. Hence funding the metaverse would be a collective effort, and several companies have donated funds in this regard. In the gaming sector, Epic games have donated over $1 billion to fund the development of the virtual world.

One sector of the metaverse that most investors have spent more money on is the cryptocurrency economy. Several firms have launched cryptocurrencies that will be used in their virtual world. Blockchain technology will allow for commerce and transactions with the virtual world. Blockchain technology will also help for data continuity on the platform.

The identity of the users will not change but remain constant no matter where they are on the metaverse. For instance, the identity of a person in the Fortnite game will be the same in the Roblox universe. Also, the commerce and advertisement sector will change totally. This was confirmed by Brian Biggot, the co-founder of Octi.

Octi is a startup that is working on a social metaverse. Augmented reality can be used by companies to make transactions a very social experience. For instance, instead of the conventional tracking of websites visited by a user to know the kind of ads to display to them, companies can use what users are building to know the kind of ads to shoot at them.

Another sector of the metaverse that will need funds is the networking sector. This is because the current bandwidth is very slow and cannot handle huge traffic. High-speed connections and bandwidth will be needed to improve the experience. As a result, there should be huge funds for that sector to improve computing power so that millions of users can have a smooth virtual experience simultaneously.

Facebook has donated $50 million for the development of the metaverse. The name of the fund is called XR Programs and Research Fund. According to the social giant, the funds will be used for external and programs research for the next two years. Before this, the company had provided funds for academic research. This research will look into how AR headsets and VR hardware will affect the social well-being of users. According to the company that is now rebranded as Meta, the virtual world is the next big computing platform and researchers, policymakers, and other industries will have to work together to build it.

Facebook noted that the goal of the funds it has donated is to build its section of the metaverse while looking out for other services it can work together with and safety, economic opportunity, and privacy. At the moment, the biggest program of Facebook as regards the metaverse is Horizon. Horizon is an upgrade to the Oculus app and allows users to engage in virtual meetings.

Right now, Facebook's largest metaverse program is Horizon, which is available as a beta Oculus app and allows people to hold VR meetings. The developers of the Pokemon Go game have also announced their investment of $300 million. The metaverse while Kucoin labs gave out $100 million

Funding to metaverse startups so far

Gaming received most of the funding for its metaverse project. This is because of how interactive gaming is. Most people love the gaming industry and see it as a point of entry into the metaverse.

The game companies that have received funding include Genopets (NFT game), Sandbox (a decentralized platform), and Mythical Games.

Several companies have adopted the word "metaverse" into their description. 43 of these companies were founded last year, 2021. The companies are in the CrunchBase database and have raised over $96 million mostly from Series A, seed, and pre-seed funds.

Some of the recent start-ups that added metaverse to their description include:

1. Upland: The company have raised 18 million dollars from Series A funding for a blockchain-based NFT metaverse
2. Inworld AI: Inworld AI have raised about $7 million from a seed round for the development of virtual characters
3. GuildFi: GuildFi has raised about $6 million from a seed round to develop a gaming platform

What Does "Building the Metaverse" Entail?

Since the metaverse is a three-dimensional virtual world where participants can communicate or interact using avatars. Originally, the metaverse was imagined by Neal Stephenson in his book. He described the metaverse as an escape from the real world. One would ask, what does it actually mean to build the metaverse? Unlike virtual reality applications, the metaverse is more than a software that can be manufactured using the normal development model.

Rather, the metaverse is a complex Virtual environment that depends on 7 distinct layers, as suggested by Jon Radoff. Jon Radoff is the author of the book "Building the metaverse." It is, rather, a complex digital environment built on seven distinct layers (suggested by Jon Radoff, author of Building the Metaverse blog. Below are the seven layers upon which the metaverse will be built:

1. Infrastructure – technologies for Connectivity such as Wi-Fi, 5G, cloud, and hi-tech materials like GPUs.

2. Human interface – haptics, VR headsets, AR glasses, and other technologies users will leverage to join the metaverse.

3. Decentralisation – edge computing, artificial intelligence, Blockchain, and other democratization tools.

4. Spatial computing – 3D modeling and visualization frameworks

5. Creator economy – A collection of digital assets, design tools, and establishments of digital assets and e-commerce.

6. Discovery – A content engine driving social media, reviews, ratings, engagement, including ads, etc.

7. Experiences – Virtual Reality equivalents of digital apps for events, work, gaming, shopping, etc.

Currently, over 160 companies are working on one or more of these seven areas.

Who will build the Metaverse?

As of this moment, different companies are working tirelessly 5o build the new foundations for such a multidimensional edifice. For instance, Epic Games developed Fortnite in 2017. Fortnite allows players to take part in various okay modes and includes a “battle royale" mode. In the battle royale mode, about 100 players can fight head to head in a Last man standing kind of battle. When the company was asked if Fortnite was a platform or game, the owner Tim Sweeney referred to it as a game and told the interviewer to ask that same question in a year. In the months that followed, the company worked on fortnite and evolved into a world that had its own money, population, and economy. The difference between both worlds was blurred. For instance, popular rapper Travis delivered music concerts with over 50 million users on the platform. And by the way, Epic is not the only company that views gaming as a medium into the metaverse.

Amazon owns Twitch, a live gaming platform with more than 140 million monthly users who have watched almost 2 billion hours of live content as of

April 2021. Other brands have noted this and are currently working on their own platform. In 2020, Burberry live-streamed its latest fashion collection on the Twitch platform, making it the first to do so. The live stream had an audience of about 40,000 viewers. It would be wrong to think that Amazon does not have the facilities and tools to compete with the metaverse.

Another online gaming company is Roblox. In 2020, more than half of United States teenagers under 16 years of age played the game. One difference between Roblox and other gaming platforms is that the users are responsible for building the games using simple developer toolkits made available on the platform. This user-generated approach has made it possible for the game to have millions of games in just a short period. Roblox is currently a small economy of its own where there are content creators who can monetize their created games by adding virtual goods and upgrades as part of the game. Players can purchase these upgrades, and when they do so, the proceeds are shared between the creator of the game and Roblox. In certain cases, top creators could earn as much as $1 million each year in physical cash.

Another platform is Facebook which has bought into the idea of the metaverse due to its huge potential. This is shown in 2014 when they acquired Oculus, a developer of virtual reality headsets. Recently, Facebook also created a platform known as Horizon, which is still under beta development. Horizon will allow users and small groups 5o to engage and interact in different experiences and activities. Users will be able to enter a virtual, real-time life version of Facebook. Like Roblox, the company believes that organizations and users will be responsible for developing the landscape of the platform.

The main point is that the metaverse will be developed by a collective effort and not by one company or individual or group of individuals. Brands, individuals, technology companies, governments, and NGOs are the parties that will be involved.

Though companies such as Google, Amazon, Disney, and Facebook, will build their presence on the metaverse and seek to dominate, they must all agree on sets of protocols and rules for how operations and activities will occur across all domains. Also, there will be protocols for how various devices can access the metaverse. From this discussion, we can see that the metaverse will only come to actualization when these platforms such as Fortnite, Horizon, and others are brought together into one universe where individuals can teleport seamlessly from one experience or world to another within a few seconds.

Economic value in the Metaverse

How can a person or company create something of economic value with a digital world?

In the real world, what governs the value of any object includes some parameters such as ownability, scarcity, and authenticity. Before now, the internet has been without boundaries and has a limitless content supply. This limitlessness is what has commodified digital products. The internet was made as a place to share files and not to buy files.

Let's take the example of LeBron James. How much is one highlight video of the basketball worth? If it is something I got from YouTube, it is not much since there is no unique or limited information about it. It is everywhere, and everyone has access to it. Anyone can simply download the same video, and nobody owns it. Yet, if you check NBA Top Shot, one highlight video of LeBron James is selling for over $230,000.

NBA Top Shot is a platform where investors and fans can sell, buy and trade sports videos that are officially licensed. There is a small difference between the expensive chip on NBA TOP SHOT and the worthless video clip from YouTube. Top Shot authenticates each clip and assigns copyright ownership to them with blockchain technology. This is not the same as the clip that was obtained from YouTube.

In the same way, any digital asset such as a piece of art, clothing or photographs, or experiences can be authenticated as a genuine asset with blockchain technology. These authenticated assets are limited in supply and have ownership. As a result, these unique limited assets carry a certain value depending on how rare they are. These assets are known as NFTs. Let's use Pokemon cards, for example. The cards do not have any value in themselves. It is only rare and authentic cards that command extra value. This same rule now applies to various digital assets, the first of its kind.

Currently, more than $100 billion have been realized from the buying and selling of NFTs. Today we have the sale of collectibles and digital art. The market is gaining worldwide acceptance and popularity.

An example is the case of a digital artist named Mike Winkelmann. Winkelmann works under Beeple and has never received up to $100 for his art piece. At the end of 2020, Winkelmann sold an NFT of one of his pieces for over $66, 000. A few months down the line, this same piece was sold for about $6.6 million. You can see the huge price gap and difference. Also, in 2021, Winkelman sold another piece of art through Christie's auction for $69 million. You might be wondering why the huge price difference. The price gap is huge because the art is authentic, has ownership rights, and is rare. The rights of the art piece can be verified using a blockchain ledger.

These economic principles are entering into other virtual goods such as collectibles, clothing, and, even recently, virtual real estate. There are platforms such as Upland where individuals and businesses can buy virtual real estate land for a certain amount of money. An example is the case of the New York Stock Exchange, which was sold for $23, 000. Who would spend such a huge amount of money on something that is not real but a digital representation? The person that is capable of making such an investment is someone who believes that as people invest and assets become scarcer, the price of digital holdings will rise. It is just the law of demand and supply.

Can Specific Territories Be Attributed to Building the Metaverse?

This question is relevant because experts have developed this theory that the metaverse can operate independently as a nation with its own population and economy. Most of the companies and firms we have discussed are from the US, UK, and Eu. But China is also making waves into the metaverse. They have gained an edge in building a sophisticated World.

While the majority of the companies we've discussed are based in the United States, the European Union, and the United Kingdom, China is also making inroads. The country has steadily gained an advantage in developing sophisticated AI, and the majority of VR manufacturing is done in China.

You are the central piece of the Metaverse Puzzle

The easiest way to build a successful metaverse is to increase user-generated content.

This leads to a single conclusion: user adoption, and eventually user-generated content from you, is the key to building a successful metaverse.

Facebook's meteoric rise is inextricably linked to the growth in user numbers, as is the case with Microsoft, Decentraland, and others. And this is most likely the most difficult obstacle of all. It's been nearly three decades since the internet's inception, and we're still far from reaching full Web 2.0 adoption. As the metaverse is built, stakeholders must focus on lowering adoption barriers and addressing user apprehension.

The Players (Metaverse Companies)

Other than what the metaverse is about, there is also the question of who will build the metaverse. Will various companies have their metaverse, or will the metaverse be one giant community?

Who will build the metaverse?

It is impossible to place the ownership of the metaverse into the hand of any individual or organization. This is because the metaverse is a democratized and decentralized concept. Hence, no company will solely own the metaverse. The metaverse belongs to everyone, and it's every person's responsibility to build it. Multiple organizations, grassroots creators, and developers will build the metaverse. Below are some companies already working on the metaverse and investing in it.

- Facebook
- Microsoft
- Roblox
- Apple
- Minecraft
- Epic games

Facebook (Meta)

Recently, Facebook rebranded itself and changed its name to Meta. This action was for the company to realign its goals and investment with whoever will build the future. "Facebook" as a name did not resonate with the visions and goals of the company. The company is currently trying to enter the virtual world by setting up a virtual reality program called Oculus. This program will bring the virtual world into social networking.

Facebook has about seven of the structures needed to build the metaverse. With the company's facilities on the ground, a prototype of the metaverse can be built and managed for the next 2 to 5 years. Facebook has an Oculus headset and a good economy.

Below are some notable projects that the company is currently working on as regards building the metaverse:

Project Cambria

The company produced a virtual reality headset that is compatible with their Oculus program

Virtual Reality messaging

This will help to connect different users in a brand new way. Messaging will take a new shape when this is finally launched. We can only observe how things unfold.

Horizon Marketplace

Meta is building a store where creators, buyers, and sellers can come together to exchange digital assets. These digital assets will be of use in the metaverse.

Zuckerberg, CEO of Meta, has also talked about how important cryptocurrencies, blockchain, and NFTs (Non-Fungible Tokens) will be in the metaverse. Paper currency can not be used to buy things in the metaverse; there will have to be digital currencies that will serve as legal tender for transactions. To this note, Meta has been working on Libra; a cryptocurrency used to make purchases in the metacommunity. Perhaps, the company is looking for some way to introduce their Libra project into the future.

Epic Games

This is the company that produced the popular virtual reality game Fortnite. Fortnite is a very developed game. The game has turned into a huge social platform with more than 350 million users. Virtual reality events include brands, celebrities and concerts, and award ceremonies; epic Games have always shown interest in building the metaverse. The company provided $1 billion as funds to fuel the development of the metaverse.

The company's major goal is to expand the game Fortnite to support more than 65 million users every month. Also, the company wants to develop the 3D, VR, and AR content so it will be more accessible. To get an interconnected metaverse, the ecosystem also has to be developed. Users of the platform can now create three-dimensional content that will improve the game's general usage.

Microsoft

Over two years ago, the pandemic came and sent everyone indoors, away from their schools and workplaces. Learning and communication had to happen online. This is part of what prompted the company to invest in the metaverse.

Though it was great and exciting to communicate with work colleagues through the internet, meetings and other conferences became impersonal. Most workers went into depression because they started missing out on the small discussions and moments they enjoyed at work, such as interactions, catch-ups at the car park, etc. All these prompted the company to start developing the virtual platform.

The tech company Microsoft is approaching the metaverse from a work angle. The computer giant wants to connect all its offers into one digital environment. The environment will be called Mesh. Inside the environment, users will be able to access Windows, Microsoft Teams, and other Microsoft services in virtual reality. VR headsets and mixed reality glasses will be used for this purpose.

Users can enter virtual meetings, talk about shared documents and files, and carry out other activities. Team meetings will have an animated whiteboard, photographs of clients, and highlighted tasks. The technology that can access the software includes laptops, smartphones, or VR devices. The software will be based on the company's mesh technology.

Roblox

Robox is a gaming company that is based on virtual reality. The company announced that they are working on a metaverse that will meet players' needs and provide tools to ensure the metaverse is safe for everyone. Roblox started recently and is already a popular platform where users can play games.

This is an example of a pre-metaverse that allows its users to invent virtual worlds build games they like that will be available for other users to take part in. Chipotle has noted that it's launched a restaurant in Roblox, which is the first of its kind. Even popular rapper Lil Nas X had a metaverse-based concert on the Roblox platform.

However, their plans of launch in China may be difficult due to the regulations there. Roblox is willing to comply with the laws there because its fan base in the country is very high.

Minecraft

Minecraft has been around for years now. The game is similar to some digital Lego that has infinite possibilities. The game developers invented it in the 2000s to serve as an extension for some browsers. Fans of the game could build anything they wanted using three-dimensional cubes within a digital space. Also, the game had an option if players wanted to stay alive. All the players had to do was feed, gather resources, and escape being killed by deadly creatures in the game.

Though the game started small, it has grown massively. It currently has fast servers that are highly populated and offers several mini-games, projects that allow users to build anything they want. Minecraft also has colonies of different people in tribes where they have specific roles to play for the betterment of the tribe. All this started from just saying a simple block game and has turned into something huge.

Why Minecraft is considered a metaverse

The first criteria for an ecosystem to be considered a metaverse is that an individual must be able to be in a virtual space and experience the things that are in reality digitally in the virtual world.

Minecraft can carry this out using various mediums. Also, the person must have a role in the metaverse. This role will depend on their server and the metaverse they are assigned to.

Minecraft allows its users to invent and design their metaverse the way they want. This is an open end game and can be customized. For instance, if a group of people creates a server whose goal is to stay alive and create a new generation, that is metaverse.

How do NFTs fit into the metaverse?

So what are NFTs?

To understand what non-fungible means, let us look at the meaning of fungible. Fungible means it can be replaced with another of the same kind. That means N500 is fungible since it can be exchanged for identical bills. Cryptocurrencies are also fungible as you can replace a Bitcoin with another one. This is different for NFTs because it is the opposite. No two NFTs can be the same. When NFT is created on a blockchain network, a unique ID is made and linked. So, it's the same for art as no two art pieces are exactly. NFTs allow artists to earn little from their art if it is sold. In so doing, if their work becomes popular and skyrockets in value, they won't be left out.

Non-fungible tokens (NFTs) have a crucial role in using the metaverse. NFTs refer to a secure kind of digital asset based on blockchain technology similar to cryptocurrencies use. An NFT can represent a song, digital real estate, a piece of art, etc. The NFT is copyright or proof of ownership that can be sold or bought in the virtual world. This is one reason several notable celebrities and public figures are converting songs and albums to NFTs. Even automobile companies are now converting their car models into NFTs. Examples of brands thinking in that direction include Lamborghini, Ferrari, Tesla, and Nissan. According to the Chief Executive officer of ORE System, blockchain and NFTs lay the foundation for virtual ownership. He also believes that NFTs are the vehicle that will help to transfer one's identity in the physical world to the virtual world.

Definition Of NFT

An NFT is a stored data unit on a blockchain technology that acts as a digital ledger and can be traded but is not interchangeable. NFTs could be photos, audio, and videos. Since each token is unique and has a set of codes to identify it, it is different from blockchain cryptocurrencies like Ethereum and Bitcoin.

Characteristics of NFTs

1. An NFT refers to a data unit stored in a digital ledger known as a
2. blockchain. The NFT can be traded or sold.
3. NFT can be linked to a physical or digital asset and the license that specifies what the asset can be used for.
4. An NFT can be traded on a digital market.
5. NFTs are copyrighted properties

Function of NFTs

NFTs are similar to cryptographic tokens, different from cryptos such as Ethereum or Bitcoin. Since NFTs are not interchangeable, they are not fungible. For instance, all Ethereums are equal, but every NFT might represent a different asset value. Non-fungible tokens are made when blockchains are in a set of cryptographic hash, a set of characters that identify a set of data, onto old records, thereby producing a chain of data blocks that are identifiable.

This process of cryptographic transaction makes sure each digital file is authenticated by making available a digital signature that can be used to track ownership of the NFT. Nevertheless, data links that show details of where the digital art is stored could be affected by what is called link rot.

Reasons why NFTs are Valuable

One advantage that NFT has over fiat currencies is that its value does not fluctuate according to the exchange rate in the global market. Scarcity, certificates, and history are factors that affect its value. The tweets of Jack Dorsey are being sold at a high price because it is rare and desirable. Another benefit that increases the value people place on NFTs is speculation. The value of NFTs can change over a while, and this will mean huge returns for those who purchased them at a low price

The Connection Between NFTs and The Metaverse

The major connection between them concerns digital assets and how they will be valued. The virtual world will let users showcase digital arts, and nfts will allow them to place a price on the content. NFTs will also provide them with proof that they are the owners.

NFTs use the same blockchain technology that is used by cryptocurrencies. NFTs are not currencies themselves. Each NFT is attached to a particular item which could be a piece of music, video, painting, or anything that can be attached to that time. NFTs have become a new way for artists and musicians to retain ownership of their work and monetize it.

Several NFT markers are available where individuals can buy these tokens and sell them. The optimal currency used on the metaverse is NFTs because of the technology they are built on and how they will allow for identity and ownership. The potential that NFT has in the virtual world is limitless and very attractive. The topic of NFTs is a huge topic of its own. There are several advantages for the use of NFTs. Further benefits will roll out the moment the metaverse begins operation.

At the moment, NFTs are very popular in the gaming sector. Different games have released their own NFTs, which users can get either by earning or during auctions. The gaming opportunity has well received the new initiative of incorporating NFTs into the gaming platform.

How will NFTs Impact The Metaverse?

NFTs have the power to disrupt the usual user interaction, socialization, and means of transaction in the digital world.

1. It will lead to a fair and open economy

Currently, businesses and individuals can convert their physical products in the real world into digital assets and NFTs that one can sell on the metaverse. One way that more assets in the real world can be converted to assets in the virtual world is to introduce gaming models that use blockchain technology.

Play-to-earn games are one approach that can be used. Players will have to know NFTs to carry out transactions in the gaming economy and get rewarded when they play the game. Players will be given full ownership of their assets rather than it being controlled by a gaming entity. The value of an NFT will depend on how rare they are. For sure, the metaverse will have an economy, and the financial laws that apply in the real world will apply there, such as the law of demand and supply, the law of scarcity, etc.

2. It is an extension of the community, identity, and social experiences

Non-Fungible Tokens will play a vital role in ensuring that data continuity occurs. Individuals in possession of certain NFTs can come together to form a community that can create and share content.

The NFTs will also tell what an individual is interested in inside the metaverse. Advertising companies can use these interests to know who to target. Currently, the trending NFTs are avatars. These avatars represent an individual's imagined self from the real world. The avatar can serve as recognition that will allow individuals to access certain parts of the universe. For example, a workplace in the universe will only allow workers with the company. By using the avatar of persons on the metaverse, only approved avatars will gain access to such facilities. NFTs avatars are an extension of a person's real self in the natural world. Some of the existing avatars include cryptopunk collections and Bored Ape Yacht Club collections, which will grant the holders access to an exclusive community with locked contents and private events.

3. Ownership of Property such as Virtual Real Estate

Using NFTs, users can buy virtual spaces and lands in the virtual world to hold events or build a house. The blockchain technology that NFTs are built on will allow users to own their properties fully. It will also allow them to develop their properties as they choose.

Uses of virtual reality estate include selling land for gains, renting out land to get passive income, hosting social events, etc.

Presently, real estate is present on the metaverse called Decentraland. Decentraland hosted an exhibition of virtual clothes in partnership with Adidas. The designs of the clothes were auctioned as non-fungible tokens. Musicians and artists are currently interested in the metaverse as they can buy land, develop it and host shows there while collecting tickets as NFTs.

Though the metaverse is still in the early developmental stage, there are numerous opportunities that NFTs can be used for, and it will offer people some way to earn, buy, sell, interact and socialize.

Ownership of NFTs is very important to enjoying the metaverse. Users can start gathering NFTs now because they will be useful in the digital world and not just the real world.

Controversies Surrounding NFTs

1. Conspiracy about its Origin: The origin of NFTs and what they mean can easily be changed or destroyed by users who do not like cryptos. Another person can attempt to link this exact image to

another address. This will allow for stealing another person's work.

For instance, an artist posts one of his drawings on his or her Twitter page, and the drawing does not have a watermark; any user can get hold of the image and use it to generate an NFT that certifies the image as their own. Then, the image was put up for sale in an Ethereum market, and someone purchased it; whoever buys it will be getting a pirated work without the consent of the real author. Also, the real author will not be able to sell the art as a unique work in another market.

2. Lifespan of Assets: one other weakness of non-fungible tokens is durability. They do not last forever. This is not the same for physical artworks that can stay for many years and still have a chance to be restored. NFTs are unstable and can change.

For instance, a user purchases a high-priced character of a game in blockchain, and the application is outside blockchain. This means that the app is not part of the Blockchain society. When the company goes out of existence, the user can no longer play the game, and his character will not be useful.

NFTs: A Good or Bad Investment?

Non-fungible Tokens are becoming an acceptable means of exchange between buyers to sellers worldwide. However, most persons believe that NFT is nothing but another digital image. There may be some accuracy in this, but one advantage is that you can sell it several times. Thus, when you invest in NFT, you gain ownership and access to a real asset. From the above discussion, we can say NFTs are a good investment form over a long time.

How can you have an investment in NFT

There are different ways you can invest, but one is to put your money in projects that have a token. In other words, you commit your money to different cryptocurrencies with NFT tokens, which allows you to profit by trading over a long time. Some examples include;

Flow (FLOW): This is a decentralized blockchain. It is known as the basis for a recent race of applications, digital assets, and games that empowers developers to create a crypto-enabled business.

Decentraland (MANA): This is a decentralized VR world. The players here are allowed to have and trade virtual lands and other non-fungible tokens.

Enjin Coin (ENJ): Their goal is to produce the best way humanity can use Blockchain technology and create an advanced economy that is not centralized. Enjin houses different applications designed for fashion, real estate, virtual earth, digital identities, gaming markets, and future virtual worlds.

Proof that an NFT Market is Efficient and has a bright future.

The development of the NFT marketplace is a good idea as it can produce steady revenue. According to estimations, from 2019 to 2020, capital increased from $141.56 million to about $338.04 million. Some Proof that shows how efficient and successful the NFT marketplace is are given below:

The real tweet of the successful Jack Dorsey was sold for about $3 million.

The Top shots of NBA, which is a trading card system (TCS), is worth about $230 million at the moment.

Earlier in 2021, the Track Kings of Leon was sold for over $2 million.

Another outstanding deal is CryptoPunk #6965, worth more than $1.54 million.

For February, the sales of OpenSea's were more than $95 million.

Even if the cost of many goods and their demand should drop, NFT products will always remain in high demand, mostly the arts and games. The proofs above are testimonies to this fact, and therefore NFT market is highly recommended.

Characteristics of NFTs Market

It's possible to base NFTs on different items ranging from collectibles digital assets to gaming assets. A developer of NFT can produce an infinite amount of tokens. Below are characteristics that both differentiate and explain NFT markets:

- Tokens have affiliation
- Tokens cannot be imitated
- Tokens are rare
- Ownership gives more power
- Conformity
- Clarity

Another reason anyone should consider being involved in the development of the NFT market is that it is simple to transfer and trustworthy.

How the NFT Marketplace Operates

The transactions that occur here depend on smart contracts, which refer to an agreement that shows the terms of the transaction between a buyer and seller. This info is usually encoded inside a smart contract then kept on a network. Bitcoin and smart cards have the same working technology.

How to Launch an NFT on the Marketplace

There are lots of business opportunities here, and below are some things to take note of;

You must know your target market and develop them: NFT markets have different niches. So, you must know who your target customers are and carry out campaigns geared towards attracting them.

Be prepared for challenges that might come up: You need to do a thorough research to know the different challenges that users might encounter when using the market for the first time. This will make for a smooth experience.

Choose the right strategy for your market: You. must know the integral characteristics of your proposed NFT business. Some amount of expertise on technology is needed to do this. So, you have to get these people and work with them.

How close is the metaverse?

The technology needed to access the metaverse is unavailable to everyone. This can only be changed when tech giants join the trend. This will mean improving the hardware (data gloves, glasses, and headsets) used for AR and VR. Also, the space will have to be improved using apps and software.

The hardware that will allow people to do business virtually or hang out will also need to be developed. Both Microsoft and Meta have their respective glasses or headsets, and Apple is allegedly working on its first VR/AR headset that will be released soon. This development will also creep into workplaces and offices, but it will take various years of investment before we can start reading the joy of the metaverse.

Though the idea of connecting on a virtual space has been around for centuries, a real metaverse where social connect and animated interactions are possible is yet to come. As noted by Bill Gates, co-founder of Microsoft, most people are still yet to have motion capital glovers and virtual reality goggles. These are devices that will help capture the body language, expressions, and vocal quality of users. Gates believes that most virtual meetings will no longer be 2D but 3D with all the participants displayed as virtual avatars in the years to come.

What Does Metaverse Work Look Like?

The metaverse is a three-dimensional space where participants can interact with one another and with the environment just like it is in the physical world. Platforms with features similar to the metaverse already exist, such as AltspaceVR and Decentraland. These platforms allows it's users to create several VR spaces or rooms for multiple purposes. This is not the same as the vision for the metaverse as put forward by Meta and other theorists. A real metaverse will be a single platform converged and operating across different worlds. This will have effects for professional use. For instance, the metaverse may have cityscapes and office campuses where different employees can meet or carry out tasks. The virtual environment will have an infinite whiteboard, teleportation, 3D data modeling and simulation, and lots more.

When can we expect to see it?

According to the CEO of Meta, Mark Zuckerberg, it would take about 5 to 9 years before the metaverse will be launched. At the moment, some aspects of the metaverse are currently in existence. Tools such as virtual-reality headsets, online worlds running for hours, and ultra-fast broadband speeds are available at the moment and are in operation already. They may be inaccessible at the moment but would be soon.

Is the metaverse here yet?

The metaverse is not here at the moment; it is still under development. This is the metaverse's early stages, with huge opportunities and prospects.

The opportunities are limitless, and it is a good opportunity for companies looking to invest in the virtual world. The metaverse requires some infrastructure and facilities before it can begin operation. So, we will not be wrong to say that the metaverse is a future dream that will soon be achieved.

What is the metaverse like right now?

The metaverse is still a dream that various brands and companies are working to actualize. Hardware and software are being produced at the moment in preparation for the metaverse

CHAPTER THREE: New business models and opportunities in the virtual economy

The Dangers of Running An Organization in the Virtual World

Doing business in the metaverse entails some risks. Offering new business segments or investing in new channels necessitates large sums of money. Especially since the metaverse is still being built and business ideas are still being developed. Therefore, the investment capital is at risk but on the other side of the risk are huge business opportunities. The blue ocean strategy, which provides real benefits and usage for users, has the potential to generate a significant advantage over competitors.

Creating new channels and technology is a risk, especially since experts predict that the metaverse will take years to become mainstream.

In comparison to the total number of social media users, VR headset technology is not widely used. Different users may react differently to VR. As a result, this company may not see as many customers as expected. Businesses may have difficulty achieving universal reach.

Another major concern for businesses developing new business models is the possibility of cryptocurrency value fluctuation. All business transactions in the metaverse will use blockchain, either through cryptocurrency or non-fungible tokens (NFTs). Because the value of cryptocurrencies varies greatly from day to day, there may be some economic instability in the metaverse's business and revenue. Furthermore, major investments made through NFTs may not be as dependable as real-world trades. For example, despite having legally paid for the work, the buyer of an NFT may be unable to edit it. This may deter certain customer types who want more freedom in using their new product.

Another issue relies on the portability to the physical world that applies the risk to metaverse native businesses. They might find themselves restricted to a small fraction of the global population to VR infrastructure and other internet or technology-related issues.

What makes the Metaverse so appealing?

From a technical standpoint, blockchain gives all digital assets executable property rights. From the standpoint of Internet development, 3D and multimedia have always been the general trend. The Internet has evolved in a more vivid direction, from text messages to pictures to videos and live broadcasts. Metaverse combines two points of view: it is built on blockchain technology and adheres to the general trend of rich content. So, what business models will exist in the future Metaverse?

Possible Businesses In The Metaverse

The selling of Clothes

The selling of digital clothes can be the next big game in the metaverse. Have you ever wondered what avatars will be wearing in the metaverse? This can be a good opportunity for smaller enterprises who are ready to work on it.

This is because it used a personal 3D printed garment and accessories, which are available in great supply due to the number of factories worldwide that are providing products of good quality. It is like a company that is producing physical clothes.

The machine for carrying out 3D scanning or garments is cheap and can be obtained from factories. The development of a 3D scanning machine will make it easy for enterprises to sell offscreen clothes online by paying a little fee for each print.

Big companies are not the only ones fighting for a spot in the clothing sector. Small businesses such as Telenitri are asking competing. Telenitri made some accessories Tango smartphone owned by Google. Telenitri has opened w store in IMVU where its users can order virtual products at particular prices. The company also produces personalized prints and is estimated to earn about 10 cents from each product.

Also, you can build a clothing brand inside the metaverse with the aid of EpiProdux's tool. This tool is helpful and can be used to plan for events, including time for a campaign, and set up distribution channels that can allow you to begin making a profit. EpiProdux can guide you on starting and managing a clothing business in the metaverse.

Construction

Owners of land with several plots but little time to build it can hire professionals who will complete the job from design to construction. This will help to boost their brand and give them more credibility. Examples of such third-party firms that engage in construction in the virtual world include LandVault, V3VA, and Voxel Architects. They help landowners to build on their land.

These developers are selling virtual equipment and tools and are also looking for clients in metaverse platforms such as OpenSim. They have designed and produced plans of buildings of various sizes. These houses can be bought on OS Grid.

Sales of NFTs Sales

This is a famous business model and is one of the oldest. The common formats used were auctions and galleries with customers buying Non-fungible tokens and popular artists selling their music or album as NFTS. Using this format, artists can have a gallery in the virtual world where they can sell NFTs to customers who need the 3D models.

Artists on the metaverse are currently making virtual objects from materials such as minerals for sale at an auction or replacing existing designs.

Currently, accessories such as that of Rose Jewelry will replace rose petals and Zero QC

Examples of prominent galleries include Cryptovoxels, Song Ting's Panda Gallery, and BCA Gallery.

You can build and even manage NFTs sales models using aEpiProdux management tool. Customers can use the tool to provide support for customers by segmenting them.

EpiProdux has a great dashboard where artists look to manage their customers, sales pricing, and inventory management using the price comparison on several other markets. You will be able to calculate the margins, price of items, cost of printing, etc.

Vox Sales Business Model

Unlike what is obtainable in the real world, the materials used for the virtual world are different. For example, VOXEL is made up of voxies. Destroying a unit of VOXEL will leave only the raw materials. All users must have a vox to display their avatar or their dress-up venues.

Unlike the real world, the materials used in the virtual world are different. For example, VOXEL is made of voxies. Then, buildings are composed of voxies. Whenever a unit is destroyed, only the raw materials remain. All players must have a vox that will be shown to their avatar or dress up venues. Vox merchants are those that sell vox. Merchants can sell it and certain other goods.

Merchants buy voxies and other kinds of goods from sellers. They have a storefront that is 2D and a virtual world where the shop must be set up. The shop will have products related to the liking of avatars. Most sellers use coal, gold, or iron ore and product colors like cashmere for avatars dressed like pandas by Song Ting, the owner of Panda Gallery.

Merchants can also sell products to customers either by logging in to Meta and selling straight from the store page on Metaverse or by drafting orders from 1 to 800 numbers. Merchants can also add everything together to get the cheapest combination and then ship all of them (Securitize).

Examples of Vox merchants are Vox Shop, Metaverse VoxWalk, Uniqlo, and Panda Gallery.

EpiProdux is a wonderful tool that can be used to target potential customers and close deals. It is a profit-driven product tool that will help you know about your real profit and the kind of product you can have. EpiProdux also has handmade tools that give its users a picture of the sales process. You can also use it to target campaigns for more sales and analyze key metrics such as market share or profitability.

Gaming

Computer gamers use gaming metaverse to play games on sites like MOBAes.

It is typically team-based and connects players in the same way that MMORPGs do. However, it lacks real-time communication features such as voice chat and leaderboards because games are persistent within the virtual world rather than passing through servers, which takes time.

Sandbox is one of the first ones dedicated solely to blockchain gaming. NFTize voxel assets, such as CastleBlock (inspired by the popular video game Minecraft) and FunFair.

Although gamers in the space have not explicitly requested that Bitcoin Magazine build their blockchain networks, they have discovered ways to work with Ethereum's Metamask app. The app allows users to pbuxe of e NFTs without being tied to a specific chain other than Ethereuim itself.

Players enjoy playing games while also investing in NFTs. Within those virtual reality universes, one popular way to participate is to create a character, make friends, or plot romance plots.

Immersive Experience

Immersion is a user-driven approach in which games are so interactive that the user's focus is completely immersed in the game experience with almost no outside distractions.

This has been made possible by advances in video technology. Virtual reality headsets have also advanced rapidly in recent years, fueling interest among enthusiasts in playing computerized content at stores such as Oculus Rift's flagship. New technologies, particularly always-on smartphones, have also enabled people to play video games while on the go.

It must be noted that all forms of immersive gaming should mean playing games or computerized narratives. It should also include real-life elements (such as spectator sports or coaching simulations).

Advertising

VR advertising is fantastic. Because of the immersive sensation, advertising in virtual reality forms, most commonly known as "360," can be more powerful and engaging.

The Metaverse Cryptovoxels billboards service costs 1 ETH per week. This model enables small groups of users from all over the world to create advertisements. Corporations can rent out billboards in the Metaverse using blockchain technology and experiment with advertising packages to deliver results faster, more efficiently, and at a lower cost than traditional models that rely on biased editorial based on personal desires.

Provider of Data Services

Websites of Internet service providers and content owners are typically protected by firewalls. It is more difficult for them to keep up with the rapid pace of technological changes, systems, designs, and algorithms that underpin the Internet — for example, visual effects achieved through HTML5. Blockchain technology's Metaverse will make it easier to protect businesses from falling out of step with changing environments.

Data is everywhere, and of course, the Metaverse is no exception. The platform needs visitor data for each package, potential buyers need historical data on the package sold, and potential sellers want market data to set their asking price. Data support is necessary for each above, and a professional data analysis provider may become an important business.

Because the mobile internet is the universal context for personal mobility, all users must feel entitled to a high-quality mobile experience. Metaverse has enabled data service providers from all over the world to consolidate their offerings on a single integrated platform. Also, this has created new business models in data-related fields:

1) Data exchange among different user sessions for a better mobile experience

2) A better experience will be a go-to for natural data development,

3} More accurate and timely acquisition of real-time virtual reality,

4] High-quality road by given points within smart contracts,

5} Inheritance of different augmented information,

6] Real-time operations lime Gas tracking.

SimpleGeo's real-time location and tracking service is an example of a metaverse data service provider. This automatically extracts geographic data from the Metaverse. The user can request a premium subscription to use their data for 'augmented' services like voice recording with landmark suggestions based on recorded audio files.

Real Estate

Metaverse's overall growth has been driven by digital real estate, trading, and leasing. In particular, the provision of relevant transaction data to real estate developers and overall metaspace leasing has created enormous profit opportunities for service providers in a variety of fields, including residential emergency all lease agents, emergency room doctors providing medical services onsite via mobile terminals, and the installation of remote work hyper implants with AI technology embedded.

Online KTV

KTV refers to a kind of electronic music video where users. Customers can hire aby mini-structure that will listen and watch other users perform on stage via holodeck technology in a virtual soundproof room (like High Fidelity). Such stations are fully operational for different languages and were well received.

Online Education

Online learning is much of a deal now. This is because Augmented reality can be obtained

Augmented reality technology can be used for distance learning where students or teachers can show the students what they are supposed to learn in the classroom. It's only a matter of time before much is enjoying it rained, and longer have interest in the physical class

An example is the STEAMTrainer which is very interactive and not just s one-way street is the online service called zsteam. This interactive augmented reality tool provides advanced training to scientists and engineers, much like a baby hugging the chalkboard demonstrator in some more traditional environments.

Sales of goods

Mixed reality will be accessible to Commercial Enterprises and those months in the years to come.

This will help to transform lives and lead to more developmental experiences in different areas of endeavor.

The major disadvantage of today's 2D e-commerce is that these texts and pictures do not relate in any shot or the film is shot. According to a pre-adjusted situation, and because of end users' products.

On the video game Roblox, the players can create how they look and sell the look to other members. Some months back, Gucci partnered with Roblox, and they had a virtual game experience for the market.

"Fortnite" worked hand in hand with superstar Ariana Grande. Millions of users and players will grace the occasion. They will be able to purchase virtual goods from her tour and see her avatar. Also Forntite met with Balenciaga to launch a game accessories.

The metaverse will bring buyers close together and to their customers. Uses will be able to customize products to fit their taste. Also, the 3D display in the virtual world can avoid the wrong product in the metaverse. It is not only a physical product that will be sold. Physical procurement will be fine.

Data Provider

One good thing about the metaverse is the large volume of data it will generate day in day out. These data don't take long to authenticate, unlike what is seen in the real world. The data developed from the metaverse is genuine since it was gotten from the blockchain. Having such data can help you to understand how things are in the metaverse

For instance, an individual or business needs to know the shopping preferences spending power of a place to know the kind of business they will model. There could also be buyers who want to know more about a virtual piece of land. At this point, data providers will be needed that can give results. Professional data service is bound to play a vital role in the future, allowing people to get important data and information that will affect their decision-making process.

Digital leasing of parcels

This is somewhat similar to real estate in the physical world. Likewise, digital packages can so be purchased and then leased out. Most times, land owners have more than one piece of land. Most landowners do not have the time to build their land. They need someone to build it for them. This is what led to a lease marker.

Metaverse: A Futuristic Retail Example

Retailing in the Metaverse

In retail, some see ahead and believe there will be the creation of shopping venues in the metaverse. Example of such shopping venues includes stores, malls, etc. This may sound short-sighted and not logical. Why would someone transport real-life shopping conventions and concepts to the virtual space? Does it serve any purpose? What is the aim here? When the metaverse is finally launched, it will allow individuals to break away from the present function of real-life stores and move ahead into the future.

Why would anyone create a virtual representation of the Canada Goose store? In the metaverse, I can shop for a new Goose Coat inside an exploration experience led by Canada Goose spokesperson, in the person of Lance Mackey and Iditarod champion. I will be able to gain contextual knowledge of the performance and quality of the garment, order it, and deliver it to me in the physical world. I can also buy a new car inside the virtual world. I am not talking about the static showroom where cars are just parked there but a wonderful and thrilling experience where I get to test drive the car in the Metaverse. Also, I could choose a race track of my choice. Apart from that, I can receive beauty tips from a beautician I pulled from the metaverse straight into my room. Why would we use our present template of what a shop is for the metaverse in such a world where anything is possible? Store designers, marketers, merchandisers, and others have to start thinking out of the box and be innovative with their ideas on what a store could be? The possibilities are endless. Imagine a brand new shopping experience where users get to try what they want to buy before paying for it. Whether it is a shoe or a wristwatch, users get first-hand experience.

We shall spend time learning, socializing, entertaining ourselves, and working in the metaverse in a matter of time. Some persons can spend all their time in the virtual world if they feel the real world is limited, inefficient, and dull. If people spend more time in the virtual world, the ratio of virtual possessions to physical possessions will increase in no time. This is because individuals will try as much as possible to develop their virtual homes and make them comfortable for them to live in. Nobody wants to keep wearing the same virtual outfit to various occasions or parties in the virtual world. People would want a change of clothes, accessories and even cars.

Over the years, status symbols will be part of the metaverse, such as the virtual house, the virtual jewelry, the virtual cosmetics, the virtual clothing, the virtual cars, and the virtual assets an individual owns. Possessions in the virtual world will be as important as possessions in the virtual world. Different brands will work on this and create an array of virtual products that would have real-life prices.

We do not know if people will have to pay for their time on the metaverse yet. The number of hours an individual will spend online will also be seen as a status symbol. According to experts, the metaverse will help converge humanity and technology. It will also blend the virtual and real world. And though the metaverse will take decades to improve and develop, there will still be investments from top organizations made now and then to build that future.

For example, a startup company known as Scuti focuses on building the first retail market using games and allowing brands to sell. The brands will also be able to ship the products directly to the game players. This is a good idea to convert the physical retail store into a virtual one.

Another startup that is planning on building CGI experiences and environments for beauty and fashion brands is Obsess. There are also companies such Ikea that employ augmented reality to allow its customers to design their virtual space using Studio app. L'oreal is a beauty giant that has built a line of different virtual cosmetics. Also, Gucci that has been working on virtual clothing, has started selling already. Gucci has launched its own virtual 25 sneakers for the price of $12.99 for each pair. The designer of the shoe was Alessandro Michele, creative director of Gucci.

Though these items are limited due to the protocols and technologies we are currently using, it is still a huge step towards improving the metaverse. With time, more growth will be recorded. There will also be improvements by users and developers from time to time.

Smart brands will buy virtual estates now and have builders developing them. Having your brand on the metaverse is an added advantage as you can get both physical and digital products to the consumers who are able to share their time between both worlds. Brands that fail to develop and join the trend will be left in the boring internet and the real world.

Future Retailing: Shopping Using Avatars

Users of chat rooms and Online gamers have understood the importance of digital avatars either as an image or a representation of a person in the virtual world. Online users can shop and interact with products using digital avatars of their choice or design with the metaverse. For instance, you go into a virtual store and interact with the products there and other buyers using a virtual avatar. This will be a unique experience.

More than this, the future of retailing using the metaverse would allow users to shop using avatars and shop for the avatars like getting a new dress, makeover, hairdo, etc. There will be stores in the metaverse that would offer users the opportunity to beautify their online personality to reflect their physical body or idealized self better.

Also, vendors of physical products may add digital gears for avatars that qualify for it to blend the virtual and physical world.

Shopping in the digital world may be new to several people, but different companies and brands are already embracing it. Retailers are already taking advantage of the improved features of virtual reality gears to improve their shops so users can check out products in the virtual world and have them delivered to them at home. Example of such retailers includes IKEA and Amazon. They have invested in Augmented Reality (AR) so users can visualize digital items with their phones and visualize them on the physical body or offices or homes.

Also, brands such as Louis Vuitton and Gucci are selling digital accessories such as handbags, jewelry, shoes, watches for virtual avatars.

Other companies such as Alibaba have introduced virtual shopping to improve their customers' experiences. Shoppers can utilize VR headsets to explore the items in a virtual store similar to a physical store. This will provide customers with the experience to keep them with the brand.

Minting Teenage Millionaires

Many games are created on the Roblox platform every year, and most of the fund generated through selling the digital items, assets, and upgrades goes to the developers behind it. In certain cases, teenage game makers have turned out to become millionaires

For instance, 16years old Ammon Runger and his partner, 23 years old Stefan Baronio, have made 6 figure salaries by producing the game Mad City. This game has attracted over 200,000 players every month. MrBaronio was able to pay for college and purchased a new car. According to him, the experience is life-changing.

This is a great opportunity for teenage developers looking for ways to make some cool cash. They can create their own games on platforms and get paid when people play them.

Roblox is one platform where developers can independently create games that are popular among children. This video game has the potential to be one of the widest visions of the virtual world.

At the beginning of 2021, many people spent more than 10 billion hours playing the Roblox video game. This is from the earning report released by the company. Also, over 42 million users have logged in every day, with players spending about $652 million on Roblox. Roblox is the site currency that players can use to buy weapons, hats, digital items, and hot air balloons. After the company went public on the 10th of March, it's valuation increased to over $45 billion and is increasing every day.

At one time, a digitalized Gucci bag was sold on Roblox for over $4,100, which exceeds the product's price.

The crypto industry has produced thousands of millionaires and a good number of billionaires in the past 12 years. Many of them didn't get rich from money but early investments in BTC, DeFi, and ETH. Now, there set of people are now the millionaires of the present decade showcasing their wealth all over social media.

The wealth of these individuals are tied to crypto and the virtual world rather than physical things. There is also the case of individuals who buy NFTs when they are of little value, and boom, their price goes up suddenly, and they are millionaires. The youngsters of the present generation are shifting from the "old system" of making money to the "new system."

Gaming and metaverse crossover

The gaming sector is an important part of the metaverse and has received most of the funding so far. When it comes to virtual reality, gaming is one aspect that many people would want to experience. Even early games in two-dimensions such as Second Life and Minecraft had added elements of the metaverse into their gaming community, such as observation, 3D avatars, and world-building.

Recently, organizations such as Epic Games and Meta are attempting to build a virtual world, and gaming will be an integral part of that world. A recent survey shows that 59% of experts believe that gaming will dominate the entire virtual reality investment for the next decade. 64%also believe gaming will have the most benefit from virtual reality. Let us dive into how gaming would be like in the metaverse.

What would Gaming look like in the virtual world?

As we earlier defined, the metaverse is a unified virtual reality space where different users can communicate with one another and their digital environment using advanced human-computer interaction (HCI) software and hardware. This will widen the scope of gaming to greater heights that no one has ever imagined.

Currently, there are VR games available on desktop, mobile phones, VR gear to enjoy conventional video games. The major difference is that the gaming universe in virtual reality will appear in three-dimension. This will give the player the ability to turn 360-degrees and even feel using a realistic sense of perception.

If you think this is mind-blowing, wait till you see how it would look in the metaverse. The metaverse will take this concept much further. Individuals can combine several VR games to create one environment for everyone.

Using this context, below are the characteristics of gaming;

Games-as-platforms –

Gaming would be more flexible and easy to modify. Gamers can create content, build their own games, add other things to the digital world and treat the environment as a space where other activities can occur.

Social gaming –

The digital world is bound to be social, which makes it different from the internet and the normal VR experience. Playing games with multiplayer will occur on a different level. Friends will be able to invite their pals in the real world, communicate with them and build relationships, etc

Play to earn –

Play-to-earn will form an integral part of the metaverse. In addition to following the rules and a storyline, players can become profitable online. An instance is selling the assets won inside a game to other players for a certain fee.

There could be portable gaming assets

The architecture of the virtual world may allow for the portability of assets. Avatar upgrades or weapons obtained in one game can be moved to a different gaming environment. NFT rules will help to maintain ownership. This would be amazing to experience-Weapons from one game being operated in another.

Mixed reality experience –

The virtual world will use MR and AR to provide a better experience. There is the chance of a mixed reality where players move from a group text in AR to MR card game in a seamless flow.

Companies Changing the Metaverse's Gaming Future

The metaverse has already attracted lots of investment. The metaverse is indeed the future of gaming. Examples of the key movers in the gaming sector are Decentraland, Epic Games, Meta, Sandbox.

Decentraland

This is among the companies who bought the idea of building a metaverse. The online game has a three-dimensional Virtual Reality platform with a large area of real estate. The cryptocurrency used on the gaming site is based on an Ethereum blockchain.

Also, the company has invested in Decentral Games to help improve its gaming capabilities and to ensure its users always get the best.

Sandbox

This is also an online video game where players can create, play, govern and own a given space. The game's economy depends on the cryptocurrency and assets generated by the community. Sandbox also partners with brands to help improve its delivery and experiences.

Presently, its market has more than 20,000 NFTs users who can buy and add to their VR world.

Epic Games

This company is responsible for producing Fortnite. Fornite is a virtual reality game and also an event destination. Fortnite has become so popular that various artists have hosted concerts on its metaverse-like world.

Meta (formerly known as Facebook)

Although Meta is new to the metaverse, it has a gold virtual reality headset innovation record. The company built a universe around its Oculus products. These products show the interest of the company in the metaverse.

One such creation by Meta is Horizon Worlds. Developers can use it to create games and then publish them in the metaverse.

Issues surrounding gaming that needs to be addressed

Right from time, virtual reality and video games have always had to deal with ethical and legal issues. The same baton will be passed to the metaverse.

Below are the three major concerns that need to be looked into:

1. Services that are appropriate for children

Monitoring the activities of children is not an easy task to do. Also, differentiating a child from an adult is difficult when looking at the person's avatar alone. Games need to have controls and modalities that would ensure age-appropriate activities.

2. NFT ownership rights –

The rules and regulations governing the ownership of assets obtained in games are unclear. NFTs that are won in a game may be difficult to move from one game to another game. Also, it is important to explain the ownership rights so users will know how to use, trade, and sell their NFTs.

3. Infrastructure shortcomings –

The metaverse requires a wide range of interoperability to run, which has not been achieved yet. Patent holders and tech companies will have to collaborate to see how they can make such functionality available. Also, countries need to adopt a singular set of laws that govern activities and operations in the virtual world.

Why are established brands jumping in?

In these past months, there has been various news about the metaverse and what it offers to humanity. Mark Zuckerberg's frequent discussion on the topic has made it even more popular. Different companies are betting on the metaverse by investing large sums into it.

According to Bloomberg Intelligence, this virtual world has many prospects both socially and economically. Experts believe it would have reached a valuation of 800 billion a few years from now, and by 2030, it would be at 2.5 trillion. These numbers are enough reasons why these companies fight for a spot in the new universe. Tech companies are striving to gain enough ground in the metaverse before their competitors get in.

No brand wants to be left behind because the world is developing every day, and soon the current systems and technology will go into extinction, paving the way for new ones.

Firms want to carve out a niche and a name for themselves, apart from the money that can be amassed. One will be wondering if these companies are not afraid of losing their money in the metaverse.

CHAPTER FOUR: Introduction to decentralized worlds

As we await the opening of the metaverse, other companies are already tapping into its potential and giving users a glimpse of what the virtual world would be. Some of these worlds are highlighted below;

Decentraland

The company was part of those who started working on the metaverse very early. They e even went as far as adopting it as a core product. Since Decentraland started in 2017, the gaming platform has gained users and credibility. Someone recently paid $2.4 million for a virtual estate on the platform.

Decentraland refers to a digital world or virtual platform which brings social elements, NFTs, cryptocurrencies, and virtual estates together. The game was launched in 2017. The owners of the game are Esteban Ordano and Ari Meilich. Also, users have a say in how the platform is ruled. Just like most online games, Decentraland uses

Ethereum blockchain technology. The collectibles on the platform are represented by "collectibles." The platform's cryptocurrency is known as MANA and can be used to purchase art, land, or perform upgrades. On Decentraland, players can create content and applications and then monetize them for others in the community to buy. Players get to buy and sell NFTs virtual estates and interact with others as they play the game. An example of items that can be bought on the platform includes virtual land, sold as Non-fungible tokens (NFTs) through MANA. To develop the virtual land, players can use the editor present in the game or import three-dimensional models from software such as Blender. Users can also buy hats and t-shirts.

Axie Infinity

Axie Infinity allows users from across the globe to earn tokens as they play the game. When users receive Axies as a gift, players can settle touching the Smooth Love portion. When these tokens are sold, can someone make about 300?

Although the game does not have an avatar or character that members can use, it allows users to have a metaverse-like job: Sky Mavis, a Vietnamese studio developed by the game. Just like the first game, Axie works on an existing product in the market. Players can collect, breed, raise, battle, and exchange creatures called Axies. Most of the players are majorly from the Philippines. This report was made available by CNBC in 2021. Many Philippines looking for ways to earn extra cash spent so much time on the game. Last August, the Department of Finance in the Philippines classified the cryptocurrency from Axie Infinity as security that should be taxed.

Players interested and want to participate in the game have to buy at least three axies. According to a 2022 report, Sky Mavis estimated the amount spent by an average player on the platform to be $1000. Users who want to earn the cryptocurrency used on the Axies platform have to pay for the starting costs first and then play the game to earn tokens. Tokens are cashed out every 14 days. The game has been reported as having an unstable market that depends heavily on new players' recruitment. Other users on the platform can buy virtual lands in NFTs and other game assets.

What makes the game interesting?

The game takes the fun and interesting part of Pokémon and mixes them. The Axies usually yield good results: Smooth Love Potion (SLP); several players have spent quality time on such platforms to earn big. The way the gaming economy is going, we are headed towards an economy owned by players and will depend on activities to remain relevant.

There is a program where Axie scholars such as Yield Guild Games and a host of others take part, and Axieowners loan out non-fungible tokens to players to use to earn. The profit realized is divided amongst those involved.

SuperWorld

SuperWorld is currently building a community in Augmented Reality that will be powered by blockchain technology. The company has built an AR real estate market plus the Advertisement market on its blockchain. There will also be an Augmented social Reality which will allow users to make their real-world by putting things like photos, 3D objects, texts, videos anywhere and sharing using the AR experience with other users.

SuperWorld refers to a virtual world present in augmented reality that is digitally mapped over the earth's surface. Plots of land on SuperWorld are represented using NFTs corresponding to the physical world space.

SuperWorld is an AR world mapped geographically on the real world, allowing users to invent, discover and even monetize AR content. The real estate of SuperWorld allows its users to buy digital plots of land worldwide, share in the generated revenue, and become an important stakeholder of the platform. After users have bought virtual lands, they can choose to resell it later for a fee or keep it and get a future share of AR digital commerce, advertising, data analytics, and e-commerce revenue generated on that piece of land. The platform has a mobile application that users and brands can design in the real world to make it more personalized. We are currently waiting for the app to be released on iPhone.

Cryptovoxels

What is "Cryptovoxels"?

Cryptovoxels refers to a metaverse and virtual world that runs on an Ethereum blockchain. Players can buy land, build stores, and even art galleries. The platform also has avatars, text chat, and avatars that are inbuilt. Below are the activities that users can carry on the platform and decentralized economy:

- Create avatars
- Build stores
- Create and develop an art gallery with NFTs

- Buy virtual land
- Interact with other users
- Play games that are developed especially for the platform.

Inside Cryptovoxels, there is Origin City, and the owner is "The Corporation." Some individuals own parcels of land. Landowners are free to create blocks, build on the land, remove blocks and even add certain features such as images and audio. There are times when individuals can give up their land for community development. To buy land on Cryptovoxels, you need to have an ETH wallet.

Cryptovoxels mixes gaming and DeFi. This is common with most universes and games inspired by the metaverse.

The Sandbox

This is a decentralized ecosystem that is community-driven. Here, creators can share and sell their voxel assets and gaming experience on the Ethereum-based blockchain.

With the aid of free software on Sandboxes, such as Game Maker and VoxEdit, game designers, artists, and players can make Assets and game experiences, art galleries, and dioramas for themselves and share with other players. These assets can be sold to get passive income as the creator.

Also, Sandbox has a market for NFT where users can publish, upload and sell NFT creations made using VoxEdit. First, the creations are uploaded to an IPFS network to serve as decentralized storage. Next, they are registered on the blockchain to show ownership. After this is done, the creations are now assets that can be sold by first placing a sale offer on the market. Potential buyers will now bid for the price or purchase at the stated price.

Sandbox uses different types of tokens to make sure the economy remains circular between users who can engage with the platform. The user types include landowners, curators, creators, and players.

Some terminologies in the Sandbox are;

SAND: This is an ERC-20 token that is used in the game as a form of payment and interaction in the ecosystem.

LAND: This refers to digital or virtual real estate on the platform. Users Can buy land which they can populate using interactive experiences, assets, and games. Each LAND represents a non-fungible token that is on the game's Ethereum blockchain (ERC-721).

ASSETS is the token created by users who either build or assemble user-generated content (UGC). ASSETS are built on the ERC-1155 standard. Also, they can be traded on the market, and their main use is to serve as elements of creation in the Game Maker.

Somnium Space

This refers to a virtual world that is built on the Ethereum blockchain. In this virtual world, users can buy parcels of land, import or build NFTs, trade, and even explore. Participants can join the platform from their mobile devices by visiting the website or downloading the app on a computer for participants to join the platform. After doing so, they can now enter into the virtual worlds using virtual reality headsets such as VIVE, HP, HTC, and others.

The Token used on Somnium Space

The token used in the game is CUBE, an ERC-20 token. Players can use the token to buy virtual assets and pay for services on the metaverse, such as renting land and paying for events and games. CUBE can also be used to reward good players.

Users can store CUBE in a digital wallet and a custodian like Gemini.

Somnium Space is a digital universe that allows users to transit into a virtual reality experience. The game is built on an Ethereum blockchain, and the main use is to allow players to buy digital land, create a custom home, construct high buildings, and trade digital assets in the game that have special value in the online metaverse.

The creator dynamics and tools provides users the opportunity to project, construct and also trade cities, township, and megaprojects while walking around in the arena of other participants

You can imagine people entering a shopping mall, seeing a movie, eating in a good restaurant, or renting a house. The good part is that you get paid each time any user visits your virtual world

There are limitless possibilities and tons of opportunities to either create, construct, and monetize creative skills and imagination. The game does not make use of sub-servers. Somnium Space hosts all players in one huge universe unlike the conventional multiplayer virtual reality game.

In that space, the users can invent surroundings, environments, and arenas which can be customized, programmed, and deliver great virtual experiences.

NFTs are responsible for powering the game to create and trade assets in the market inside the virtual world and ecosystem.

Presently, Somnium spaces can operate using 4 elements which are:

Software Development Kits (2011) helps users create and develop their properties, avatars, and gifts land.

Virtual Reality Experiences this is a builder module that is complete and helps users to create digital structures and environments that will make it fun

NFT market – this helps monetize and trade digital properties that the players created.

NFT-based assets - Helps for incorporating NFT assets from the whole blockchain universe to be used in Somnium space.

A guide on how you can invest in the metaverse

An individual can choose to invest directly or indirectly in the virtual world. There are three methods to invest in the virtual world directly.

Direct ways of investing in the metaverse

1. Buy metaverse tokens such as MANA or SAND

2. Buy NFTs inside games

3. Buy Virtual land

Indirect ways of investing in the metaverse

An individual can buy stocks associated with the metaverse, such as Facebook or Apple. Another way to invest indirectly is to put money in a virtual world index.

CHAPTER FIVE: The Metaverse Economy

What Is the Virtual Economy?

A virtual economy refers to one that exists inside a fantasy, usually a gaming world. The different economies are majorly found online in real-time virtual worlds or multiplayer worlds. Virtual economies use virtual currencies, although these currencies cannot be traded for real-world currencies in a bank.

A virtual economy is similar to a real economy, although some differences exist. Most people interact in the virtual world to escape from their everyday life and have fun.

Some factors, such as the need to buy food, buy electricity, be attacked on your way back from work, will not happen in a virtual economy. An avatar usually represents people that play online games. These avatars help to safeguard the identity of the person behind them. The avatar is not restricted the same way humans are in the real world.

The resources available to these avatars are different from what is under the possession of the human counterpart. The property that might be found may be more or less similar to that in a real-world economy.

In a game, one player can purchase a country cottage that looks like that could be bought in the real world, and in another game, a floating castle. There are some features that the fantasy-based world shares with the physical world, such as the right of people to own things and do whatever they want with them. The market value of something is based on its use and how people want it.

In more famous games, they want Items just like wanting new ones. This real demand is the connecting bridge between a real and a virtual item. Although the games have prohibited such actions, some players now pay real money to buy online game resources and currency.

Virtual economies have been existing even before the inception of the internet. Card and live role-playing games involving economic transactions provide players with points or digital money.

Inside card games, most players have attached a large value to rare or useful cards. This is a predecessor to the current and growing phenomena of real money being spent and earned on virtual resources.

A Design Strategist at the company known as Seymourpowell, Dave Ralph, gave some reasons why brands should start considering the virtual economy as a source of revenue now and in the future.

The first time you must have encountered virtual economy must have been on your credit card statement. Many small transactions are charged by a company you don't know of. When you finally connected the dots, it turned out that it was something that had to do with your Minecraft obsession at a young age.

Dig deeper a little bit and see that the digital space is not all for hardcore gamers and teens who pinch credit cards. It is becoming a viable channel and opportunity for big corporate brands and consumer brands to promote new products and monetize them. From Gucci down to Verizon, brands that we know and like are embracing a new virtual way of consumption. Everyone is joining the idea, including parents, celebrities, and teenagers.

How to get involved as a Brand

Similar to the world of gaming, the virtual economy is not yet taken seriously by several brands, even with huge prospects. It is still a world of strange names, words, trivial things to buy, and all for many. This is an attitude that must change.

The upcoming generation will see the theory of virtual consumption as something important, even more than the things they buy in the physical world. This is why brands must see this huge opportunity and the opportunity to make good use of it. There are many opportunities here that can take any business to the top in years to come. The CEO of Gucci made a statement at an opening ceremony in Florence. Marco Bizzarri noted that the company wants an early start before other brands see the huge potential it has to offer. At the moment, it may not be a huge source of income but could bring more opportunities in the future.

How should traditional consumer brands examine the potential of putting money in virtual experiences or products in this new and virtual economy? Below are three strategies that represent the steps needed for a conventional product to enter into a virtual economy.

The Step: The brand has to provide good digital content tied to their service or product experience.

An initial introduction to digital asset creation for virtual stages shouldn't be something you charge clients for. It's more about fostering your playbook and getting where your objective purchasers may be and what they esteem. It can begin with something as straightforward as a Snapchat Geofilter, an area-initiated channel for the famous social media application that clients can access at areas of their decision. Mcdonald's, Starbucks, and General Electric have all made interesting channels attached to stores, areas, or seasons of day, which clients can get to when they are nearby a geotagged area.

Verizon built a virtual NFL arena inside the Fornite Creative Mode universe as a feature of its Superbowl LV enactment crusade for a bigger scope. The arena could have 50 fans all the while and permitted clients to take an interest in virtual meet-and-welcomes with avatars of genuine NFL players, as well as contending in select smaller than usual games all through the arena.

Moving into the virtual economy involves carrying out average advertising methodologies of restrictiveness, access, and local area through these current computerized stages. Which stages you pick are not entirely set in stone by your objective purchaser's digital habits.

The Stretch: Create digital twins of products or merchandise and sell them within virtual world economies

The virtual world offers the opportunity to play imaginatively with actual properties in manners that resist this present reality's regulations (or complex preferences). The inventive ventures of style and plan are driving the way in enhancing inside this space.

Gucci has been at the very front of trial and error with virtual style resources, in a longing to catch the consideration of hyper-picture cognizant, social media hungry Gen Z shoppers. Not just has the brand digitized its whole coach index for virtual take a stab at in the Gucci application. Yet, it has likewise delivered a restrictive computerized just mentor - the Virtual 25 - planned by Gucci Creative Director Alessandro Michele that individuals can take a stab at utilizing expanded reality and "wear" in photos for social media. At $8.99, this computerized coach is a take when contrasted with a genuine pair of Gucci's that retail for upwards of USD 500.

Digital artist Andrés Reisinger shot to popularity recently when things in his assortment of "virtual furnishings" sold for many dollars each utilizing virtual resource closeout site NiftyGateway. For Andrés, the unbounded imagination stood to him by the virtual world permitted him to configure pieces that highlighted peculiar, gravity-resisting structures in extravagant materials and completions that would be incredibly difficult to duplicate. Winning bidders had the option to outfit their virtual homes by transferring their furniture to virtual stages like Minecraft.

To succeed, this methodology requires more noteworthy responsibility and assets. Gucci's virtual economy is an installed divert in their retail procedure and a long-term interest in advancement. While making advanced resources for sale shouldn't be costly, any brand should initially contribute time to comprehend the basic innovation, client typologies and commercial center elements of likely virtual stages, while building relevant associations with the gaming organizations that own these platforms.

Leap: Use blended reality technologies to blur the lines between real and virtual world experiences of your product or service

This last method is to a greater degree of where things might head, as blended reality advances multiply and the lines between the genuine and virtual universes become progressively obscured.

Streetwear celebration ComplexCon's 2020 occasion was held inside a customized virtual world called ComplexLand. Guest avatars could enter the world and buy genuine streetwear things in coordinated drops around the virtual space, tune in on talks and boards, and request food at virtual food trucks. Yet, a long way from essentially being served virtual grub, the coordinators empowered a genuine food request to be conveyed to members' homes promptly after putting in a request with the virtual road merchant. It's not hard to envision organizations like Deliveroo and Just Eat opening up virtual "eateries" later on that satisfy genuine and virtual hunger.

The following boondocks utilize tactile brain science to enhance genuine encounters through shading, fragrance, and sound. Driving the charge in this space are exploratory eating encounters made by gourmet specialists, such as Mattia Casalegno, whose AeroBanquets RMX blended reality feasting experience serves little courses to cafes who experience holding eating the dishes inside a VR universe. This approach discards the tangible shows of food utilization, permitting cooks to play with our impression of taste and smell through the impact of shading, sound, and moving pictures.

Although this space is in its early stages, the quickly diminishing expense and mainstreaming of VR and blended reality headsets will open doors for brands to investigate the tangible increase of genuine item encounters inside our homes. It may not be some time before you are tasting your cherished natural tea, drenched in a virtual climate that utilizations tone and sound to unwind and quiet you while upgrading the kinds of the blend

Career Opportunities in the Metaverse

Something beneficial about the metaverse is that it considers old positions that are currently changed and makes ready for new ones that never existed.

Some of these jobs include:

Metaverse Properties

An organization referred to as metaverse properties prides itself as the primary computerized land organization worldwide. How the organization treats go about as a specialist or agent between the purchaser and the vendor. The firm works with the rental or punch of land or property in different virtual universes like Upland, Sandbox, Somnium, and Decentraland. A portion of the organization's administrations incorporates artistry displays, family, homes, and business spaces.

The metaverse has opened doors for old and new organizations like Metaverse Properties. Other new organizations will likewise come up later on. As of late, Nike purchased RTFKT. RTFKT is a new business that makes virtual shoes and advanced ancient rarities utilizing blockchain validation, NFTs, and increased reality. This is a splendid move by Nike as it sets itself up for the computerized world. Nike has likewise cooperated with Roblox on "Nikeland." Nikeland is a virtual existence where Nike fans associate, mess around, interface even dress avatars in various virtual attire.

Stylists and personal shoppers

The virtual space will have its shopping centers, retail regions, and arcades. Individuals will search for garments or wear for their avatar in shopping centers. This is because appearing in the virtual world is just about as significant as appearing in reality. For this situation, individuals can deliver administrations like individual customers and beauticians to help clients look great and drive deals for firms working in the Virtual world.

Tour guides

Virtual amusement parks are one spot where avatars can visit the metaverse for diversion and media. Organizations, for example, Disney, are chipping away at a venture along this line. Virtual reality amusement parks will require local escorts to talk with clients and show them around. Complex Virtual Reality conditions from verifiable landmarks historical centers to carnivals will require local area experts, and this is an open position for those intrigued.

Artifact hunters

There could be a work situation for hunters in the virtual world who might assist clients with tracking down uncommon resources in games

Metaverse games could drive monetization for players

Recall play-to-earn games; this is an incredible chance for clients to mess around and acquire from them. Relic trackers will likewise be paid when they can find ancient rarities

Top 5 Metaverse Stocks to Buy for the Future of Technology

Fastly

Metaverse sector: Infrastructure

Market value: $6.3 billion

Cloud computing and decentralization have made a slight issue: inertness or information slack. Clients experience this constantly, clicking a connection on their web program and trusting that the following page will download or interaction to occur. The distance the information needs to travel isn't anything to joke about if they're looking into the climate. However, assuming they're in a self-driving vehicle or performing an automated medical procedure, the information slack can be something beyond a migraine.

That is the place where edge figuring and innovation organization Fastly (FSLY, $49.79) comes into place.

FSLY works an edge figuring foundation as-a-administration (IaaS) stage that carries servers and other gear to the wellspring of information creation. Fastly's foundation can move 145 terabytes of information each second across 28 nations. It decreases the slack time and inertness of decentralization.

Organizations appear to like the company's contributions. Income development at Fastly has been quick since its send-off 10 years prior, with incomes developing 14% year-over-year in the last quarter.

Like distributed computing, the metaverse will require many edge registering answers to get it going. Contemplate the sheer measure of information move expected to make a virtual world progressively that clients will communicate with. Without edge registering and organizations like Fastly, such exchanges can't work.

Notwithstanding its possibilities as a metaverse stock, FSLY also makes an intriguing development play on the proceeded extension of distributed computing. But then, Fastly shares exchange at not exactly a large portion of their 2020 top around $125, so financial backers can catch them with quite a bit of their foam knocked off

Nvidia

Metaverse sector: Infrastructure

Market value: $745.0 billion

Nvidia (NVDA, $297.52) has often been promoted as one of the most amazing semiconductor stocks to purchase for the long stretch. Not amazingly, its introduction to the universes of artificial intelligence(AI) and other quick handling chips make it a strong player in the realm of metaverse stocks.

NVDA's chipsets are observing their direction into different servers, and other brought together PCs expected to run complex estimations. That incorporates edge processing stages run by firms like Fastly. With this administrative role and the need to move rapidly, Nvidia is nearly destined to be a top champ from the metaverse unrest.

Also, another explanation for its future looks surprisingly better: is its forthcoming buyout of ARM Holdings from SoftBank Group. ARM is a huge player in-licenses and programming that permit chips to be carried out into PC frameworks. NVDA will want to work out its start to finish environment with the buyout. It can put its graphics processing unit (GPU) and progressed chips into more frameworks straightforwardly and support registering power. Furthermore, the metaverse will require this sort of processing ability to work.

And keeping in mind that it's generally $40 billion buyouts of ARM are everything except guaranteed - with U.K. controllers among the latest to raise antitrust worries - NVDA is as yet a possible champ from the metaverse. Its chips keep on turning into the norm concerning rapid computations and processing

Roblox

Metaverse sector: Virtual platform

Market value: $47.5 billion

A video game appears to be an odd decision for design house Gucci to send off a restrictive occasion, yet it goes to show the forthcoming force of the metaverse and how Roblox (RBLX, $77.99) is building this future.

By all accounts, RBLX is a video game. An extremely famous one at that. The organization has 43.2 million day-by-day dynamic clients who logged 9.7 billion hours of commitment in the subsequent quarter.

The thing is, it's not a solitary game. Roblox utilizes outside engineers to construct different games, content, and other diversions for its clients. The firm brings in cash by selling its virtual money that players can use to get to these games, encounters, content, and surprisingly virtual attire - like a Gucci sack - for their characters.

Roblox has made the base for the metaverse inside its game. Furthermore, it's growing that further.

In the organization's new income call with experts, Roblox CEO Dave Baszucki referenced that the association's foundation "invites six-year-olds and, simultaneously, invites 30-year olds." Ultimately, Roblox considers its foundation to be a virtual spot where these vivid encounters, as are shows, are "going on constantly, similarly as play is going on constantly at this moment," Baszucki said.

To get this going, RBLX is going through a few oodles of cash-on ability and acquisitions to work out its variant of the metaverse. A great representation is its new acquisition of Guilded, a stage intended to associate different gaming networks.

Concerning the actual organization, Roblox keeps seeing expanding incomes from its foundation and plan of action. The firm understood an astounding 126% year-over-year bounce in deals for its most recent quarter. This follows a 140%

year-over-year income expansion in the principal quarter.

Given its administrative role in the underpinnings of this next rush of innovation, this metaverse stock could be a strong decision for portfolios

Meta

Metaverse sector: Hardware and apps

Market value: $934.3 billion

Mark Zuckerberg and recently renamed Meta (FB, $341.13) set up for the company's metaverse vision back in 2014 when the organization bought VR startup Oculus. All in all, FB struggles with the division as far as its social media tasks, and it generally appeared to be a prevailing fashion business for the firm. Yet, Zuckerberg may, at last, be triumphing when it's all said and done.

FB sent off a public variant of another Oculus application called Horizon Workrooms in August. Utilizing the company's VR headsets, clients can partake in meetings through avatars. They can see their PC screens consoles and even take an interest in virtual whiteboards.

"Later on, cooperating will be one of the fundamental ways individuals utilize the metaverse," Zuckerberg wrote in a new blog entry. Also, Facebook seems to be one of the first to carry such apparatuses to the market. Given the new flood in telecommute courses of action because of COVID-19, this positively could be a significant win for Facebook in the close term.

The organization's greatest suggestion to the metaverse to date came in late October when Facebook reported the alteration of name to "Meta Platforms, Inc.," or only "Meta" for short. Likewise, the stock will change tickers, from FB to MVRS, on Dec. 1. While Facebook and many of its other applications will keep up with their names, Oculus will be rebranded as Meta.

FB is an assortment of networks through its different applications and corresponding stages, so the metaverse checks out for the organization to turn to.

Over the more drawn-out pull, this could bring an auxiliary stream of promoting income or expenses for content makers inside its foundation and framework. That is far off; however, given the metaverse stock's administrative role in equipment and current first-mover status in applications intended for work, Facebook could arrive sooner than others.

Even better, FB addresses a protected play on the development of the metaverse. There's no denying the association's benefit or income age. That could give moderate financial backers genuine serenity as they look toward the subject.

Autodesk

Metaverse sector: Software

Market value: $70.1 billion

Autodesk (ADSK, $324.52) opened up to the world, thinking back to the 1980s, and is most popular for its spearheading AutoCAD programming. This application permits engineers, planners, creators, and scholastics to virtually plan and make structures, items, framework tasks, and more in both 2D and 3D. It’s the standard programming for the business, and most development projects eventually contact the product during their lifecycle.

That product is as yet the association’s meat and potatoes, assisting it with acknowledging more than $1 billion in deals during the second quarter of this current year alone.

It gets intriguing for ADSK that engineers have begun utilizing its product to plan and fabricate virtual universes for gaming and amusement. The firm currently offers a set-up of items intended to deliver 3D movement, develop and send off virtual structures, and make inside VR and augmented reality (AR) spaces. Incomes from this fragment (M&E) were up 10% year-over-year in the most recent quarter.

Autodesk is a characteristic fit and rapidly turning into the top decision for designers taking a gander at the metaverse and its development.

Maybe the greatest aspect of all of this is that Autodesk has kept turning towards a better software-as-a-service (SaaS) model, with repeating incomes representing 98% of all-out deals in the latest quarter. Those repetitive incomes have converted into a lot of benefits, too. Income flooded 23.5% in the second quarter, with ADSK delivering $186 million in free income (the money staying after an organization has paid its costs, the premium on obligation, charges, and long haul speculations to develop its business).

With a long history of 3D plan behind it, Autodesk settles on a top decision for financial backers taking a gander at metaverse stocks

How to Purchase Metaverse Land and Other Digital Items

Some virtual platforms have made marketplaces where individuals can buy and sell virtual land and other forms of collectibles as NFTs. Below is how to do buy in the metaverse

1. First, the individual must identify where he would like to buy virtual land. Different platforms offer virtual real estates sales, such as Decentraland and Sandbox. It will be worthwhile to do some research before picking one.

2. The user must have a digital wallet to store cryptocurrency. This wallet is computer software that can connect to a blockchain server and store cryptos. It must also be compatible with the blockchain technology that powers the platform the person is buying from.

3. Now, the buyer will have to access the platform's market using a computer or mobile with Internet access. Next is for him to connect his wallet to the platform. The market is usually on the website of the platform.

4. Now, buying virtual land is almost the same as land in the real world. The buyer will have to

consider the price, future value, and location of the virtual piece of land that he wishes to buy.

5. After the buyer has decided on the land, he must have the coins or tokens to purchase it. The token will be saved on his crypto wallet. The token to be used depends on the kind of platform he chose to buy land from. For example, buying land in the Decentraland will require the user to have bought MANA coins. If it's from the Sandbox he is buying land, he needs SAND tokens. To know the currency to use, the buyer can research online.

6. When the buyer has successfully linked his crypto wallet to the metaverse market and put funds in it, all that is left is for the buyer to place the bid on the said property or buy it at the stated price. The cost of the virtual land will be deducted from his crypto wallet, and the said NFT representing the value of the land will be sent to the user's wallet.

7. The process of buying other items, collectibles, or digital assets such as accessories clothing is still the same

CHAPTER SIX: The Metaverse; Advantages and Disadvantages

Benefits Of The Metaverse

Below are some of the tremendous benefits of the metaverse.

A World Without Limitations

For individuals, the circle of the meta world is like the world they experience consistently. Players experience building, driving, shooting, establishing stories, and carrying on with game entertainers' lives in computer games. Games like GTA 5 give an ongoing reenactment to the players, yet players can't feel or contact the climate in the game. Using the metaverse, players will feel the 3D virtual world, where they can meander and play out a few exercises.

Solving Remote Work Challenges

In the pandemic, most individuals working in the IT area worked at home; however, this needed genuine cooperation for bosses and representatives. Supervisors can associate with their representatives like in reality while remaining in a virtual world with the metaverse applications. Additionally, specialists can associate with their patients virtually.

New Opportunities For Businesses And Marketers

Meta is fostering a superior variant of social media stages, which will open doors for organizations and advertisers. Organizations can give continuous connection to clients to give different garments and extras a shot their avatars, carrying Virtual Reality nearer to reality

How can The Metaverse Help eLearning

Better eLearning

A student appreciates learning more with his cell phone than a book in current times. Metaverse applications can make a virtual space for understudies to walk, compose notes, and speak with different understudies, changing the eLearning business. Likewise, they can mess around in a virtual world that intently takes after the real world. Furthermore, understudies can likewise change garments, hairdos, and expressions with the proposed applications, among the different choices accessible.

Better Illustrations By Teachers For Students

Teachers broadly use video-calling applications; however, they can't offer a legitimate outline of genuine items through them. With innovations like AR, teachers can show such delineations really to their understudies. For instance, to exhibit the pieces of a vehicle, they can utilize holographic applications to mirror a 3D picture. Understudies will have a superior comprehension of logical and numerical trials.

Better Parent And Teacher Interactions

The metaverse can help guardians with their kid's presentation in organizations like schools. Guardians can go to the understudies' classes and be guaranteed the nature of schooling presented in the establishment. With Virtual Reality applications, guardians can likewise cooperate with instructors from remote places and audit the nature of the games their youngsters play. Likewise, guardians can organize standard meetings with educators and plan better eLearning for their kids

Better Learning Resources With 3D Visualizations

Utilizing the metaverse, the assets giving arrangement will be better with 3D representations. Books can be VR-upheld, and understudies can jump profound into the books, hear the text, and imagine charts in a 3D arrangement. The VR can show energized recordings to the understudies for better learning for verifiable subjects. Assessments can be more intelligent whenever joined with the metaverse applications. For instance, assessment questions can be intuitive, and understudies can be furnished with specific contextual analyses which are virtual but will feel near the real world. As such, the metaverse can shape learning assets, bringing them near the real world and making a superior eLearning industry.

eLearning applications are taking the method of gaining from disconnected to online models. With the consolidation of VR and AR advancements into these applications, we can draw one stage nearer to the plan of the metaverse. It will require almost 10 years to change the eLearning business into a metaverse.

Pros: Advantages And Applications Of Metaverse

Giant Tech has focused on creating and conveying its variant of the metaverse. Organizations, for example, Microsoft and Meta, have perceived how the eventual fate of the web and advanced correspondence is made a beeline for a more vivid computerized domain that diminishes the limits between the both world.

The center benefit of the metaverse is the distinguishing proof and acknowledgment of novel applications that would change how people utilize the web and other related advanced correspondence advances. Like Web 2.0 and social media benefits, the idea will deliver new worth making computerized items and administrations with viable applications.

Listed below are some advantages and applications of the metaverse:

Mark Zuckerberg and individuals behind Meta Platforms perceive the capacity of innovation to permit individuals to interface and communicate their thoughts all the more normally. However, current social media stages like Facebook, Twitter, TikTok, and correspondence stages, for example, Zoom, limit computerized human connection inside a two-layered plane.

Clients of the previously mentioned social media and correspondence stages are restricted to simply looking at their PC or portable screens. Be that as it may, a stage in light of the metaverse will permit a more vivid encounter by alluring a sensation of the essence. Zuckerberg calls this a typified web where the client is in the advanced insight.

The aforementioned is the motivation behind why Facebook changed its organization name to Meta Platforms and has outfitted away from being recognized as a social media organization to make a beeline for marking itself as a social innovation organization. The organization planned to join virtual reality and expand reality to empower more reasonable computerized correspondence and cooperation.

Because it is an extension of social media past Web 2.0, the particular uses of metaverse focus on making and sharing advanced data or substance that mark an emotional jump from straightforward texts, photographs, and recordings. These substances are more realistic concentrated. Besides, the participants become the content

Innovative Communication for Work and Education

The Covid-19 pandemic that began in 2020 constrained organizations from various ventures and areas all over the planet to embrace advanced advances or online-empowered types of correspondence. Remote work or working from home and work-from-home game plans have turned into an answer for keeping these organizations running and people utilized.

Indeed, even training organizations had to use advancements and administrations to empower remote or distance learning because of limitations in up close and personal collaborations. Note that the Covid-19 pandemic is the essential motivation behind video conferencing stages like Zoom Video Communications, Microsoft Team, Google Meet have become more well known.

Collaboration is restricted to screen-to-screen continuous sound and video. A stage in light of the metaverse would permit a really captivating communication among members due to the vivid and graphically-rich virtual climate.

Rather than seeing the other members on a PC screen and conveying through receivers and speakers, envision being in a virtual office or an auditorium and having the option to see around and explore through this virtual climate in a total 360-degree design while connecting with life-like avatars of the members.

New Opportunities for Businesses and Marketers

Unlike the customary vehicles of mass correspondence like transmission and print in which the crowd or bound to consume and get messages, social media's presentation and inevitable notoriety have empowered people, in general, to turn into the courier and content maker themselves.

It is also worth focusing on that social media stages have likewise opened doors for organizations of all sizes and advertisers to advance their items and administrations in manners that outperform the scope and capacities of conventional media. These stages have prepared for the presentation of a new subfield of advertising and a particular sort of computerized showcasing called social media promoting.

Because one of the romanticized uses of the metaverse is the development of social media past Web 2.0, it can likewise be utilized as a stage for showcasing. It will acquire the upsides of social media yet with more added benefits. All the more explicitly, the advantages of a metaverse in organizations and advertisers focus on the upsides of virtualization.

Advertisers can make digitized items or spot customer-facing facades in a common virtual world that clients can see and explore. It will likewise open another road for electronic business that exploits expanded reality. The associations between the objective market and promoting substance and advertisements will be more vivid. Complementing the Applications of Blockchain Technology

One more prominent benefit of the metaverse is that it enhancements or supplements the uses of blockchain innovation. Note that blockchain is the essential innovation behind cryptographic forms of money like Bitcoin, the Ether digital currency of Ethereum platform, Dogecoin, and the Ada cryptographic money of the Cardano stage.

In any case, blockchain is something other than innovation for executing and keeping up with crypto-coins and crypto-tokens. It is explicitly a decentralized or dispersed data set utilized as a record or record of exchanges. Another of its eminent applications is creating and appropriating computerized resources called non-fungible tokens or NFTs.

Through the production of NFTs utilizing blockchain innovation, a recent fad in gaming endeavors to advance the idea of play-to-procure in which players can procure a pay and secure in-game computerized resources that are tradable and usable in different stages or game titles. The type of game is called NFT or blockchain games. A portion of its remarkable models incorporates Axie Infinity.

Recollect that a metaverse is a common advanced domain of virtual space. Blockchain applications like digital forms of money, tokenization of substance through NFT, and blockchain games, as well as decentralized money and network protection, are exercises that are made conceivable through the cooperation and coordinated effort of web clients

How to create and promote a Virtual Economy

Some virtual economies exist in the present digital space. Computer games are a remarkable model. To be explicit, intelligent computer games, such as RPGs and MMORPGs, reenactment games, activity games, and surprisingly relaxed games, have inside virtual economies as exhibited through in-game obtaining and trade of in-game games resources.

A virtual economy is basically an economy existing in a virtual stage. Nonetheless, it is likewise worth focusing on the fact that virtual economies are not the same as certifiable ones. Individuals take part in virtual financial exercises for amusement and entertainment.

Thinking about the future extension of social media, the progressions to advanced correspondence, the advantages to organizations and advertisers, and the correlative effect on blockchain applications. One more benefit of the metaverse is that it can completely uphold the making of a virtual economy that capacities correspondingly to a real economy.

The metaverse will give an advanced stage to a vivid trade of computerized and disconnected items and administrations, including advanced resources. Note that these advanced resources can have true monetary worth. Moreover, it will uphold the making of new exchange exercises and occupations that exist either in the common virtual space or this present reality.

Disadvantages And Criticisms Of Metaverse

In view of the previously mentioned qualities and the benefits and uses of the metaverse, it tends to be viewed as that this idea is a common virtual space that permits a more vivid collaboration among its members. Large Tech organizations advancing its creation are focusing on individuals to live in this computerized domain.

Nonetheless, the thought doesn't agree with other industry players and pundits. It has also raised a few issues and worries because of the persevering and still-irritating issues tormenting the internet. Assuming these issues stay inexplicable, the metaverse will essentially acquire them and, in specific situations, will exacerbate them

Listed Below Are Some Disadvantages Of The Metaverse And Some Criticism

One of the drawbacks of the metaverse is that its execution will require the presentation of trend-setting innovations. There are a few advances and norms or conventions that are financially accessible to implementers. Nonetheless, the idea will require an extra interest in creating more up-to-date innovations.

Think about better web availability as a perfect representation. Taking part in a common virtual space will require solid information transmission speed since it is graphically serious. Current fiber-based broadband availability and 5G organization innovations, particularly the mmWave 5G organization innovation, may satisfactorily uphold the acknowledgment of this idea.

In any case, the reality is that dependable administrations are not open to various individuals all over the planet. What's more, tempting individuals to take an interest in the metaverse and use its advantages and applications will require a widescale arrangement of better or progressed advanced correspondence innovations by specialist organizations and important government offices.

The idea will likewise expect cutting-edge computerized specialized devices or gadgetries. These things are not promptly available to people and networks for the least difficult explanation that they either are as yet inaccessible on the lookout or stay costly. Neglecting to cause them open will to estrange a few groups from the guaranteed advantages of the metaverse.

May Harm Human Relationships and the Community

One merit of the metaverse is that it can work on the advantages of social media and existing on the web empowered method for correspondence by acquainting a more vivid way to associate and socialize with individuals on the web. In any case, various individuals have communicated worries over this implied benefit or advantage.

Previous Google CEO Eric Schmidt has communicated worry over the arrangement of Meta Platforms to present a metaverse. In a meeting with The New York Times, he cautioned that it is "not really ideal for human culture." He also said that "everyone who talks about metaverses is discussing universes that are more fulfilling than the current world."

Schmidt noticed that computerized reasoning, one of the fundamental advances for planning and running the metaverse, is a "monster bogus god" that can make undesirable and parasocial connections. He asked what might an AI-empowered companion resemble, particularly to a youngster, or on the other hand assuming artificial brainpower sees parts of reality that individuals don't.

Other business pioneers have likewise raised worries about applicable advances. For instance, in a progression of editorials posted on his authority Twitter account in February 2020, Tesla CEO Elon Musk referenced that certainty is "not high" in the straightforwardness and security of artificial consciousness inside his organization.

Prevailing and Upcoming Privacy and Security Issues

Social media sites and other online-empowered correspondence applications to incorporate the utilization of video conferencing stages like Zoom Video Communication and even web perusing have been loaded with discussions and reactions because of the security and protection hazards they posture to people in general.

These stages and applications have been condemned for being excessively meddlesome, especially because they gather a ton of information from their clients that make security and protection hazards. Moreover, this information has been gathered, sold, and utilized for nosy internet-based promotions, as well as concerning fraud and other digital-related crimes.

It is also worth focusing on the fact that a few organizations behind them have neglected to address the reactions tossed at them adequately. Meta Platforms have been the subject of examinations worldwide for their alleged inward practices that either minimize or ignore what their social media stages have contrarily meant for the interest of its clients.

Assuming the current advanced domain is as yet tormented by these worries or issues, most would agree that these will be acquired in ongoing cycles to online-empowered stages and applications, including the metaverse. Moreover, the possibility of a common virtual space will open new issues connecting with the security and protection of people as well as establishments

CHAPTER SEVEN: Crime in the Metaverse

Are we prepared to deal with crime in the metaverse?

It is now a critical piece of our computerized present reality, from ransomware assaults on people, state-run administrations, hospitals, huge companies, and even confidence associations. Nobody, it appears, is invulnerable. So one can legitimately feel that there will be a crime in the multiverse or multiverses.

Will we have a multiverse police power that can move between universes, exploring and battling crime? One can accept that certain individuals will shape their own universes inside the multiverse and lay out their own guidelines. Maybe there will be multiverse privateers who'll make their own "islands" like the privateers and pirates where they stow away and conspire, perhaps run by a Johnny Depp avatar?

While I quip fairly, it is a reasonable reality. Human practices are genuinely unsurprising and laid out. Societies might move and change, yet practices are practices, fluctuating in degrees and by culture. There are genuine dangers that misrepresentation, robbery, and harmful practices will be available. Digital money might be taken; maybe craftsmanship hoodlums will take NFT's and imaginative works. Some might game Social Tokens for their own childish and eager longings.

While there is a confidential conversation about a completely decentralized multiverse, this is just somewhat conceivable. The multiverses require a great deal of handling power and energy in true server farms. Those should work at scale and will be claimed by existing incorporated suppliers like Amazon, Facebook, Apple, Microsoft, and so forth. Then, at that point, the framework organizations like Verizon, AT&T, Bell, and others should run and deal with the links, switches, and other exhausting stuff that causes things to interface and work. So decentralization is simply conceivable to some extent. Will it be the obligation of these organizations to police the metaverse? They're attempting to do as such today with cybercrime. Will unofficial laws should be set up? How might security be made due?

These are feasible, but rather we know enough about computerized advancements today to realize that it is great but awful. Continuously. Maybe the network protection firms of today will offer metaverse-explicit crime battling administrations? How could discipline be looked for if something is taken in the metaverse? Those perpetrating the crimes may, and possible will be, situated in far-off nations. That is assuming they can be gotten.

The Problem of Measuring Crime in Metaverses

What does crime in the virtual world truly mean? This question is substantially more difficult to reply. The subject of how to define wrongdoing sufficiently is an issue not acceptably tackled in criminal science and is one that may maybe never be settled. There is a conventional thought of "wrongdoing" in criminal science: wrongdoing is conduct defined as criminal by the overall set of laws. Making a decision about wrongdoing in the virtual world is compounded by significantly more issues since such a conventional assessment is unimaginable. Second Life itself intentionally tries not to control the conduct of its avatars.

Consequently, the main choice would be to plan of action to the public or overall global sets of laws of this present reality. This would definitely bring about various appraisals/assessments since, for example, the "Auschwitz Lie" of Sect. 130d StGB - a vital offense concerning the German lawful appraisal of the Internet - would barely have a partner in different nations and would hence be of no importance for different specialists. The worldwide similarity of potential outcomes would be exceptionally restricted.

The Problem of Crime Effects in Metaverses

At last, we should investigate the people being referred to, or rather the avatars. It is problematic whether degenerate conduct in virtual universes can truly prompt such friendly harm as in reality. The prospects of exploitation are as of now significantly decreased: a manslaughter or murder offense is not really possible in Metaverses, since it is a quality of a virtual world that each member has various or even a limitless number of lives. If an avatar loses its life - and this happens all the time in numerous web-based games - it can't actually be viewed as the person in question; this is essentially not somewhat tantamount to exploitation in reality. Hence, likely violations in virtual universes lose a lot of their compromising impact. There could be impacts in the space of misrepresentation or virtual burglary. The financial action advanced by Second Life could truly be brought to a halt, assuming demonstrations of misrepresentation were completed for a monstrous scope, because genuine business visionaries would lose interest. A powerful control would be important here, and it very well may be fascinating for criminological examination to see how request could be carried to a world with a self-chose absence of rules.

Crime Incidence of Metaverses

This, notwithstanding, just addresses a little piece of wrongdoing; the sorts of violations that are especially vital to the genuine overall population scarcely assume a part in virtual universes. You additionally experience issues when you think about the wrongdoers. When an avatar is offended, who is the wrongdoer? Who should be rebuffed to the extent that it is trusted that discipline will have any impact whatsoever? What's more, if the avatar is rebuffed - there may be the chance of sending him to a virtual jail - which might really be impacted by the discipline? Eventually, the client behind the avatar is mindful, and no one but he can feel the discipline. This implies there is no discipline for the conduct of the avatar, however, just for the conduct of the individual sitting before the PC.

Subsequently, the perspective on the virtual world as an independent society is, much of the time, deficient. Just in situations where genuine social demonstrations are simply moved to the virtual world - particularly concerning trade in Second Life - would genuine social findings be able to be moved to the virtual world

Consequences of Metaverses on our Reality

Another very interesting problem to discuss concerning criminology concerns how using virtual worlds affects individuals' behavior in the physical world. About the effects of internet use on our physical life,

Concerning the topic of the impacts of Internet use, a potential expansion in the eagerness to utilize brutality - after various important cases - is at the point of convergence of criminal science and criminal strategy. Various savage demonstrations at American and European schools appear to have been motivated by PC games; in any case, it is dicey whether these are to be credited to Metaverses. This will surely become more clear in the accompanying talks. More subtle is the likelihood that Metaverses, which, as a rule, are a hoarding social counter-world, can make and focus on values and perspectives among their clients. There are reports about individuals investing more energy in virtual universes and on the Internet than in genuine societies whose social contacts are focused on the Internet. To put it plainly, individuals invest additional time with symbols than with people. These substitution universes could generally make their

values and standards. Assuming these qualities and standards oppose the qualities and standards of genuine society, subcultures arise. Furthermore, assuming these social universes have an influence on their clients, it very well might be conceivable that they will take the qualities and standards of the virtual world and apply them to this present reality. This and the subsequent conflict between the standards and upsides of virtual society and those of genuine society could influence the conduct of the clients and, likely, additionally increment wrongdoing. Up until this point, a little examination has been directed in this field, even though it could end up being advantageous.

CONCLUSION

The virtual world is the next big thing, and there is no harm if companies make themselves available on such a platform. Though nobody would own the metaverse, there will be those who will be fundamental in building it. These are important players in the virtual space and include companies such as Robox, Unity, Microsoft, Meta, Epic Games, Apple, etc. Other companies interested in the virtual world can also join later on. Companies interested in the metaverse have shown their commitment by investing a huge amount of money to make this dream a success.

Though the metaverse started as an idea, it would soon become a reality since several tech companies pool resources to provide the needed hardware and software. As was highlighted in the book, some platforms provide individuals with virtual experiences, such as Decentraland and Roblox. This will give users a feel of what to expect in the metaverse

While the virtual world is still developing, several organizations are checking out the different potentials. Examples of such companies are Decentraland and Sandbox, Nvidia, Meta, and Microsoft. Advancements in the present technologies such as Artificial Intelligence, VR, and AR, will open our eyes to more opportunities and a world without borders.

The rising interest in the metaverse stems from the recent challenges the world faced during the COVID-19 pandemic. Though the internet was available to keep us company, there was no real social connection, and this is one thing the metaverse promises us – social connection. Regarding the possible challenges and problems the platform would face, we can only hope that they are rectified as they come up. The metaverse has promising potential and is worth waiting for.

“Thank you for reading this book. If you enjoyed it, and if you want, please visit the site where you purchased it and leave a **brief review**.

Your feedback is important to me and will help other readers decide whether to read the book too.

Thank You!”

Darell Freeman

Cryptosphere Academy

www.ingramcontent.com/pod-product-compliance
Ingram Content Group UK Ltd.
Pitfield, Milton Keynes, MK11 3LW, UK
UKHW040007200726
13854UKWH00001B/92

9 798201 062651